Risk Management Handbook

2022

U.S. Department of Transportation
Federal Aviation Administration
Flight Standards Service

Preface

This handbook is a tool designed to help recognize and manage risk. It provides a higher level of training to the pilot in command (PIC) who wishes to aspire to a greater understanding of the aviation environment and become a better pilot. This handbook is for pilots of all aircraft from weight-shift control (WSC) to a Piper Cub, a Twin Beechcraft, or a Boeing 747. A pilot's continued interest in building skills is paramount for safe flight and can assist in rising above the challenges which pilots of all backgrounds and experience levels face.

Some basic tools are provided in this handbook for developing a competent evaluation of one's surroundings that allows for assessing risk and thereby managing it in a positive manner. Risk management is applied by identifying, monitoring, and managing potential components that affect risk thereby allowing the pilot to be better prepared to mitigate risk.

The pilot's work requirements vary depending on the phase of flight. As for a driver transitioning from an interstate onto the city streets of New York, the tasks increase significantly during the landing phase, creating greater risk to the pilot and warranting actions that require greater precision and attention. This handbook attempts to bring forward methods that a pilot can use in managing workload, making the environment safer for the pilot and the passengers.

Occasionally, the word "must" or similar language is used where the desired action is deemed critical. The use of such language is not intended to add to, interpret, or relieve a duty imposed by Title 14 of the Code of Federal Regulations (14 CFR).

This handbook is published by the United States Department of Transportation, Federal Aviation Administration, Airman Testing Standards Branch, P.O. Box 25082, Oklahoma City, OK 73125.

Comments regarding this publication should be emailed to afs630comments@faa.gov.

Introduction

According to the National Transportation Safety Board (NTSB) statistics, in the last 20 years, approximately 85 percent of aviation accidents have been caused by "pilot error." Many of these accidents are the result of the tendency to focus flight training on the physical aspects of flying the aircraft by teaching the student pilot enough aeronautical knowledge and skill to pass the written and practical tests. In this scenario, risk management is ignored, which can potentially lead to fatal results. The certificated flight instructor (CFI) who integrates risk management into flight training teaches aspiring pilots how to proactively identify safety-related hazards pertaining to the flight and mitigating the associated risks of the identified hazards.

A key element of risk decision-making is determining if the risk is justified. The risks involved with flying are quite different from those experienced in daily activities. Managing these risks requires a conscious effort and established standards (or a maximum risk threshold). Pilots who practice effective risk management have predetermined personal minimums and have formed habit patterns and checklists to incorporate them.

If the procedures and techniques described in this handbook are taught and employed, pilots will have tools to identify potential hazards of a flight and successfully mitigate the risks associated with the identified hazards. The goal is to reduce the general aviation accident rate involving poor risk management. Pilots who make a habit of using risk management tools will find their flights considerably more enjoyable and less stressful for themselves and their passengers. In addition, some aircraft insurance companies reduce insurance rates after a pilot completes a formal risk management course.

This Risk Management Handbook makes available recommended tools for identifying hazards and assessing risk in order to conduct the safest flight possible with the least amount of risk. The appendices at the end of this handbook contain checklists and scenarios to aid in risk management consideration, flight planning, and training.

Major Enhancements

- This version of the handbook reorganizes risk management concepts in a sequence that pilots use in real world flying.
- Chapter 1 explains the difference between risk management exercised by pilots versus a global corporate risk management system, defines the role of the FAA and NTSB, and acknowledges limits in which regulatory compliance can influence safety. This leads to the discussion of personal minimums.
- The discussion of personal minimums moved from chapter 8 to chapter 2 and is now the subject of that chapter. Since the handbook cites personal minimums throughout, the initial presentation of this concept comes earlier.
- Chapter 2 also briefly discusses the FAA's WINGS program and has a video link that explains the advantages.
- Several FAASTeam video links are included throughout the book, which explain and summarize the concepts presented.
- A unified scenario in chapters 3, 4, and 5 shows how to apply risk management concepts before flight begins and explains and demonstrates the use of a flight risk assessment tool (FRAT) in combination with the PAVE checklist.
- The discussion of identification of hazards, risk analysis, and risk mitigation has been separated into three chapters (instead of two) to clarify each step and preserve the difference between hazard and risk.
- The chapter on hazard identification (chapter 3) discusses pilot attitudes and that discussion continues throughout the book, where relevant.
- Chapter 6 begins the discussion of risk as pilots encounter it during actual flying, in terms of threat and error management, with detailed definitions and examples, and an explanation of defenses.
- Chapter 7 takes a classic look at what automation is and does, and how pilots should anticipate, act, and verify when using automation. The chapter also includes discussion of flight path management.
- Chapter 8 specifically describes ADM training. This chapter focuses on the 3P risk analysis system while in flight and moves more complex models to the appendices. This chapter also contains a real example of naturalistic decision-making and addresses CRM and SRM in more detail.
- The appendices describe and analyze accident scenarios and some provide for the reader to make an analysis.
- The appendices contain instructions for how readers may use them for maximum benefit.
- Specific descriptions of makes and models were removed since a generic description broadens the applicability of concepts presented throughout the book.

Table of Contents

Chapter 1: Introduction to Risk Management

Introduction

Pilots experience the joy of taking an aircraft and passengers on flights that are visually pleasing and productive. However, most pilots also know people who have had accidents or died while flying.

By following the principles discussed in this handbook, pilots can:

- Make safety of flight their top priority.
- Fly with confidence.
- Enjoy each trip to the fullest extent possible.

Safety Management Systems in Aviation

This Risk Management Handbook focuses on the individual and not on safety management systems (SMS). SMS addresses risk management from an organizational perspective as an ongoing activity. Interested persons may obtain information about SMS here.

Accident Causality & Responsibility

Both the National Transportation Safety Board (NTSB) and the Federal Aviation Administration (FAA) investigate aviation accidents. The NTSB determines the probable cause(s) of accidents and makes recommendations, while the FAA determines if accidents reveal deficiencies in pilot training, aircraft certification, air traffic control, or other areas of FAA responsibility. During accident investigations, the two government entities usually receive assistance from other interested parties, such as aircraft manufacturers and operators.

A review of the following accident report illustrates the role of the NTSB. The sidebar in *Figure 1-1* is an excerpt from an NTSB final report of a fatal accident involving a single-engine airplane with a reciprocating engine.

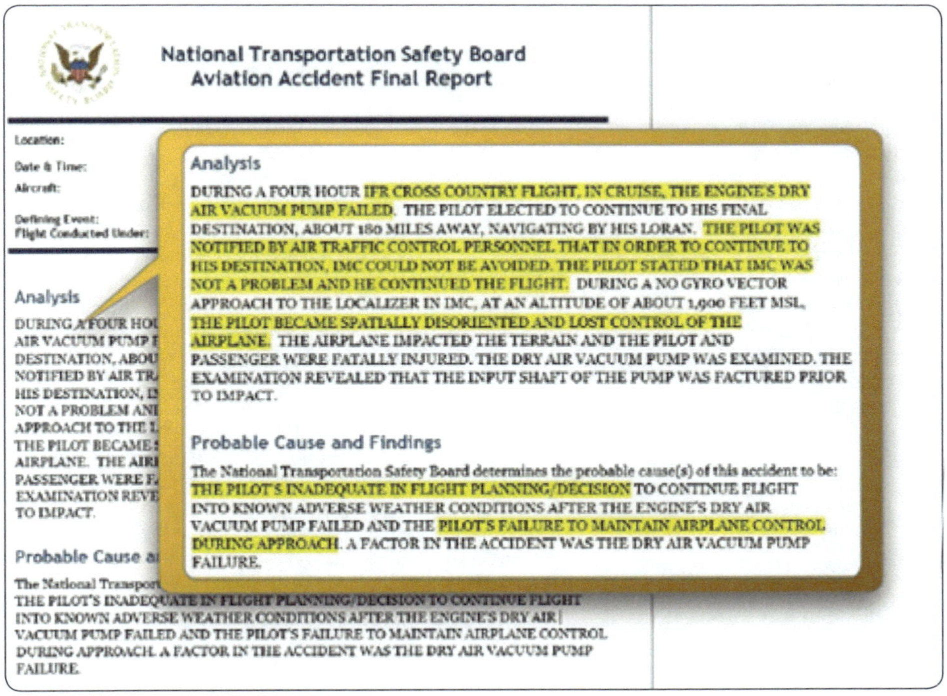

Figure 1-1. *Sample NTSB final report.*

Key findings of the NTSB aviation accident final report, highlighted above in yellow, emphasize the pilot's inadequate in-flight planning/decision to continue flight into known adverse weather conditions after the engine's dry air vacuum pump failed and the pilot's failure to maintain airplane control during approach. The NTSB report, available here, also contains information about this pilot's decision-making and risk management.

Many incidents and accidents occur as a result of poor risk management. The following accident review illustrates the importance of risk-based decision-making, as a means to prevent a negative outcome.

Risk Management Analysis Using the PAVE Checklist

The accident described above contains risk factors included in the PAVE checklist. As shown in *Figure 1-2*, the acronym "PAVE" represents hazards that relate to the pilot, the aircraft, the environment, and external pressures. The sample analysis below describes how PAVE items may relate to the accident.

Pilot

- A pilot must continually make decisions about competency, condition of health, mental and emotional state, level of fatigue, and many other variables. For example, a pilot may be called early in the morning to make a long flight. If a pilot has had only a few hours of sleep and is concerned that the sinus congestion being experienced could be the onset of a cold, it would be prudent to consider if the flight could be accomplished safely.
- A pilot had only 4 hours of sleep the night before being asked by the boss to fly to a meeting in a city 750 miles away. The reported weather was marginal and not expected to improve. After assessing fitness as a pilot, it was decided that it would not be wise to make the flight. The boss was initially unhappy, but was later convinced by the pilot that the risks involved were unacceptable.

Aircraft

- A pilot frequently bases decisions on evaluation of the airplane, such as performance, equipment, or airworthiness.
- During a preflight, a pilot noticed a small amount of oil dripping from the bottom of the cowling. Although the quantity of oil seemed insignificant at the time, the pilot decided to delay the takeoff and have a mechanic check the source of the oil. The pilot's good judgment was confirmed when the mechanic found that one of the oil cooler hose fittings was loose.

EnVironment

- The environment encompasses many elements that are not pilot or airplane related, including such factors as weather, air traffic control (ATC), navigational aids (NAVAIDS), terrain, takeoff and landing areas, and surrounding obstacles. Weather is one element that can change drastically over time and distance.
- A pilot was landing a small airplane just after a heavy jet had departed a parallel runway. The pilot assumed that wake turbulence would not be a problem since landings had been performed under similar circumstances. Due to a combination of prevailing winds and wake turbulence from the heavy jet drifting across the landing runway, the airplane made a hard landing. The pilot made an error when assessing the flight environment.

External Pressures

- The interaction between the pilot, airplane, and the environment is greatly influenced by the purpose of each flight operation. The pilot must evaluate the three previous areas to decide on the desirability of undertaking or continuing the flight as planned. It is worth asking why the flight is being made, how critical it is to maintain the schedule, and if the trip is worth the risks.
- On a ferry flight to deliver an airplane from the factory, the pilot calculated the groundspeed and determined he would arrive at the destination with only 10 minutes of fuel remaining. A check of the weather revealed he would be flying into marginal weather conditions. By asking himself whether it was more critical to maintain the schedule or to arrive with an intact aircraft, the pilot decided to schedule a refuel stop even though it would mean he would not be able to keep to the schedule. He chose not to "stretch" the fuel supply in marginal weather conditions which could have resulted in an emergency landing.

Figure 1-2. *The PAVE checklist.*

The pilot reported to air traffic control (ATC) that the vacuum pump failed while in visual meteorological conditions (VMC). As a result, the attitude indicator and directional gyro became inoperative. Rather than divert to an airport while in VMC, the pilot decided to continue toward the destination and into instrument meteorological conditions (IMC). This elevated the risks associated with an "A" hazard because of the inoperative instruments and a "V" hazard because of the IMC. After the vacuum pump failure, the pilot communicated with ATC that IMC would not be a problem, which may indicate a hazardous attitude or "P" hazard. It is unknown if an external pressure or "E" hazard factored in the pilot's apparent desire to get to the destination.

In this case, the pilot had the opportunity to change the outcome of the flight by diverting to an airport while still in VMC. Several reasons explain why pilots do not make appropriate decisions. Pilot error often results from an over-estimate of capability, a lack of preparation for flight, or a failure to prioritize safety. Varying levels of risk tolerance, or even intentional disregard of risk, may be a factor.

Risk management training includes a variety of measures that change the way pilots perceive and deal with hazards both before and during a flight. This handbook will emphasize using risk management as a process to avoid situations and decisions that might lead to an aircraft accident.

Chapter Summary

Poor risk management is a cause of many accidents. Accordingly, pilots should emphasize risk management in all types of operations, from recreational flying to using aircraft for business.

Chapter 2: Personal Minimums

Introduction

Federal regulations that apply to aviation do not cover every situation nor do they guarantee safety. For example, a pilot may legally fly in marginal VFR conditions at night even though low visibility and night hazards increase the risk for an incident or accident. Therefore, pilots should consider non-mandatory self-regulation in the form of personal minimums.

Personal Minimums

Pilots who understand the difference between what is "smart" or "safe" based on pilot experience and proficiency establish personal minimums that are more restrictive than the regulatory requirements. The following six steps allow pilots to establish a set of personal minimums in order to reduce risk and fly with greater confidence.

Step 1—Review Weather Flight Categories

Establishing personal minimums normally begins with weather, and pilots should know the range of ceiling and visibility that defines each category. [*Figure 2-1*]

Category	Ceiling		Visibility
Visual Flight Rules VFR	Greater than 3,000 feet AGL	and	Greater than 5 miles
Marginal Visual Flight Rules MVFR	1,000 to 3,000 feet AGL	and/or	3 to 5 miles
Instrument Flight Rules IFR	500 to below 1,000 feet AGL	and/or	1 mile to less than 3 miles
Low Instrument Flight Rules LIFR	below 500 feet AGL	and/or	less than 1 mile

Figure 2-1. *Weather category values for ceiling and visibility.*

Step 2—Assess Experience and Comfort Level

Pilots should also take a few minutes to complete the certification, training, and experience summary in *Figure 2-2* by filling in the right column. Some pilots fly different aircraft categories and classes and may develop different personal minimums based on the specific aircraft flown. For example, many pilots will have a different set of personal minimums when flying a single-engine airplane versus a multiengine airplane. Depending on pilot experience, the minimums in a multiengine airplane could be higher than the single-engine airplane minimums. Pilots may use the information entered in *Figure 2-2* to set personal minimums for a variety of situations using tables in *Figure 2-3*, *Figure 2-4*, and *Figure 2-5*.

Certification, Training, and Experience Summary	
Certification Level	
Certificate level (e.g., private, commercial, ATP)	
Ratings (e.g., instrument, multiengine)	
Endorsements (e.g., complex, high performance, high altitude)	
Training Summary	
Flight review (e.g., certificate, rating, wings)	
Instrument Proficiency Check	
Time since checkout in aircraft 1	
Time since checkout in aircraft 2	
Time since checkout in aircraft 3	
Variation in equipment (e.g., GPS navigators, autopilot)	
Experience	
Total flying time	
Years of flying experience	
Recent Experience (last 12 months)	
Hours	
Hours in this aircraft (or identical model)	
Landings	
Night hours	
Night landings	
Hours flown in high density altitude	
Hours flown in mountainous terrain	
Crosswind landings	
IFR hours	
IMC hours (actual conditions)	
Approaches (actual or simulated)	

Figure 2-2. *Certification, training, and experience summary.*

The tables in *Figure 2-3*, *Figure 2-4*, and *Figure 2-5* layout a sample assessment. *Figure 2-3* shows how entries might look in the Experience & Comfort Level Assessment VFR & MVFR table. Suppose a pilot's flying takes place in a part of the country where clear skies and visibilities of 30 miles or more are normal. The entry might specify the lowest VFR ceiling as 7,000 feet, and the lowest visibility as 15 miles. A pilot may never experience MVFR conditions and would leave the dash in place. However, in this example and as shown in *Figure 2-3*, the pilot regularly flies in an area where normal summer flying involves hazy conditions over relatively flat terrain and is more experienced and comfortable in MVFR. The pilot used the MVFR column to record personal minimums of a 2,500-foot ceiling and 4 miles visibility for daytime operations.

For night flight, a ceiling under 3,000 feet or visibility less than 5 miles may create an unnecessary risk, so the pilot decided to record a 5,000-foot ceiling and 8 miles visibility in the VFR column.

Experience and "Comfort Level" Assessment — VFR & MVFR		VFR	MVFR
Weather Condition		VFR	MVFR
Ceiling		> 3,000	1,000–3,000
	Day	—	2,500
	Night	5,000	—
Visibility		> 5 miles	3–5 miles
	Day	—	4 miles
	Night	8 miles	—

Figure 2-3. *A sample pilot experience and comfort level assessment for VFR and MVFR.*

For IFR, *Figure 2-4* shows how a pilot recorded the lowest IFR conditions recently and regularly experienced. Although a pilot may have successfully flown in low IFR (LIFR) conditions, it does not mean the pilot was "comfortable" in these conditions. In this example, the pilot did not fill in the LIFR boxes for known "comfort level" in instrument meteorological conditions (IMC) after deciding to avoid flight in those conditions.

Experience and "Comfort Level" Assessment — IFR & LIFR		IFR	LIFR
Weather Condition		IFR	LIFR
Ceiling		500–999	< 500
	Day	800	—
	Night	999	—
Visibility		1–3 miles	< 1 mile
	Day	1 mile	—
	Night	3 miles	—

Figure 2-4. *A sample pilot experience and comfort level assessment for IFR and LIFR.*

If combined into a single table, the summary of a pilot's known "comfort level" for VFR, MVFR, IFR, and LIFR weather conditions might appear as shown in *Figure 2-5*.

Experience and "Comfort Level" Assessment — Combined VFR & IFR		VFR / MVFR	IFR / LIFR
Weather Condition		VFR MVFR	IFR LIFR
Ceiling			
	Day	2,500	800
	Night	5,000	999
Visibility			
	Day	4 miles	1 mile
	Night	8 miles	3 miles

Figure 2-5. *Experience and comfort level assessment for combined VFR and IFR.*

Step 3—Consider Other Conditions

Pilots should also have personal minimums for wind and turbulence and record the most challenging wind conditions comfortably experienced during the last six to twelve months. As shown in *Figure 2-6*, a pilot may record these values for category and class, or for a specific aircraft.

Experience and "Comfort Level" Assessment — Wind & Turbulence	SE	ME	Make/ Model
Turbulence			
Surface wind speed	10 knots	15 knots	
Surface wind gusts	5 knots	8 knots	
Crosswind component	7	7	

Figure 2-6. *A sample pilot experience and comfort level assessment for wind and turbulence.*

In addition to winds, "comfort level" inventory should also include factors related to aircraft performance. Completing the table with reference to the aircraft type and terrain typical for most flying [*Figure 2-7*] will establish a safety buffer. If the pilot has never operated an airplane from a runway shorter than 5,000 feet, the shortest runway box should say 5,000 feet.

Experience and "Comfort Level" Assessment — Performance Factors	SE	ME	Make/ Model
Performance			
Shortest runway	2,500	4,500	
Highest terrain	6,000	3,000	
Highest density altitude	3,000	3,000	

Figure 2-7. *Sample experience and comfort level assessment for performance factors.*

Step 4—Assemble and Evaluate

Combining all these numbers results in a baseline personal minimums table as shown in *Figure 2-8*.

Baseline Personal Minimums

Weather Condition		VFR	MVFR	IFR	LIFR
Ceiling					
	Day	2,500		800	
	Night	5,000		999	
Visibility					
	Day	4 miles		1 mile	
	Night	8 miles		3 miles	

	SE	ME	Make/ Model
Turbulence			
Surface wind speed	10 knots	15 knots	
Surface wind gusts	5 knots	8 knots	
Crosswind component	7	7	

	SE	ME	Make/ Model
Performance			
Shortest runway	2,500	4,500	
Highest terrain	6,000	3,000	
Highest density altitude	3,000	3,000	

Figure 2-8. *Sample baseline personal minimums.*

Step 5—Adjust for Specific Conditions

Any flight a pilot makes involves an infinite combination of pilot skill, experience, conditions, and proficiency. Aircraft equipment and performance, environmental conditions, and external influences vary considerably. Both individually and in combination, these factors can compress or expand the safety buffer provided by baseline personal minimums. Consequently, a pilot should develop a practical way to adjust baseline personal minimums to accommodate specific conditions or aircraft.

Note that the example situations and additional safety margins [*Figure 2-9*] only provide a starting point. Pilots may develop their own adjustment factors based on experience, aircraft capabilities, and operation. If flying experience is limited or infrequent, the adjustment magnitude could increase. If multiple special conditions apply, a pilot could make an adjustment for each factor. For example, suppose a pilot plans a night cross-country flight to an unfamiliar airport, departing after a full workday. The table in *Figure 2-9* suggests raising baseline personal minimums by adding 1,000 feet to the ceiling value, one mile to visibility, and 1,000 feet to required runway length.

	If you are facing	Adjust baseline personal minimums by
Pilot	Illness, use of medication, stress, or fatigue; lack of currency (e.g., have not flown for several weeks)	Adding at least 500 feet to ceiling
Aircraft	An unfamiliar airplane or an aircraft with unfamiliar avionics or other equipment	Adding at least 1/2 mile to visibility
enVironment	Unfamiliar airports and airspace; different terrain or other unfamiliar characteristics	Adding at least 500 feet to runway length
External Pressures	"Must meet" deadlines, pressures from passengers, etc.	Subtracting at least 5 knots from winds

Figure 2-9. *Examples of additional safety margins from baseline personal minimums.*

Here are several important cautions regarding personal minimums. The pilot should:

1. Not adjust personal minimums to complete a specific flight. The time to consider adjustments is not while under pressure to fly, but rather when time and objectivity permits an honest self-analysis about skill, performance, and comfort level during the last few flights.
2. Make adjustments to one variable at a time. For example, if the goal is to lower baseline personal minimums for visibility; the ceiling, wind, or other values should not change at the same time.
3. Seek training and consult with a flight instructor before making a significant adjustment to personal minimums.

Step 6—Stick to the Plan

As many pilots know, adhering to personal minimums sometimes creates an ethical dilemma, especially when pressures exist to make a flight. Professional pilots live by the numbers, and so should general aviation pilots. Established personal minimums enable the pilot to make a no-go or divert decision rather than departing with a sense of unease regarding the outcome of a flight. In addition, a written set of personal minimums can also make it easier to explain tough decisions to passengers who depend on the pilot's judgment.

Using the FAA WINGS Program for Risk Mitigation & Safety

The FAA maintains a safety program that provides courses on a variety of topics as a means to enhance safety. The WINGS Pilot Proficiency Program is based on the premise that pilots who maintain currency and proficiency will enjoy a safer and more stress-free flying experience. As an added bonus, completion of a phase of the WINGS Program can count for a flight review and participants may receive a discount on certain flight insurance policies. Pilots may create an account and watch a WINGS video using the following links:

- FAA WINGS Program

- WINGS Pilot Proficiency Program Video

Chapter Summary

Many GA pilots have freedom to choose when and where they fly. However, this freedom may also lead pilots to situations where lack of proficiency and equipment capability become a factor. Responsible pilots set personal minimums to help reduce the probability of experiencing an encounter that could lead to an incident or accident.

A copy of the charts used in this chapter can be found in Appendix B, Risk Assessment Tools. Pilots are encouraged to copy and use the charts in the appendix or use comparable tools on an electronic flight bag (EFB) before each flight.

Chapter 3: Identifying Hazards & Associated Risks

Introduction

The words "hazard" and "risk" seem simple, but these words are easily confused. 14 CFR part 5, section 5.5 defines these two terms as follows:

- Hazard – a condition that could foreseeably cause or contribute to an aircraft accident as defined in 49 CFR part 830, section 830.2.
- Risk – the composite of predicted severity and likelihood of the potential effect of a hazard.

Simply put, a hazard is a condition that could cause an accident. The probability and predicted severity of the consequences that may result from any hazard is the risk. Identifying, analyzing, and responding appropriately to hazards decreases the risks and increases the margin of safety.

Hazard Exposure

The example of a person crossing a street helps explain the relationship between hazard and risk. The traffic is always a hazard, but it does not usually create a significant risk for a pedestrian until the actual street crossing takes place.

Some people may lack the experience needed to understand the hazards and risks associated with crossing a busy street and need to learn the procedures used to cross streets safely. In a similar way, pilots need to identify aviation hazards and associated risks and learn to deal with them appropriately. However, when assuming pilot-in-command duties, pilots encounter a variety of hazards, and they may not recognize the potential for an accident in a given situation. Pilots need the ability to perceive relevant hazards, understand and analyze potential consequences, and exercise judgment when responding to any hazard.

Why Hazards Result in Aviation Accidents

Pilots learn to recognize hazards during ground and flight training. While instructors normally include the learner in the decision-making process, training does not teach the learner how to manage every hazard. A saying goes that new pilots have a cup of luck and an empty cup of experience, and they should fill the cup of experience before their cup of luck runs out. However, all pilots should understand that any situation involving a hazard may present a significant risk to their safety. Rather than relying on luck, the correct response to a given hazard often depends on many variables and calls for a disciplined analysis and response. The following case studies illustrate this point.

A pilot with approximately 233 hours of total time rented an unfamiliar airplane for a round-trip VFR cross-country flight. The pilot had about 2.6 hours of time in the specific make and model. The NTSB narrative indicates the following:

> *According to the operator of the airplane, the pilot had difficulty starting the engine prior to departing for Erie International/Tom Ridge Field (KERI), and requested assistance. The operator proceeded out to the airplane, and showed the pilot how to start the engine. The operator then suggested the pilot leave Erie with enough time to return to Waterbury-Oxford Airport (KOXC) before sunset. Later in the day, the pilot called the operator and informed him that the airplane operated fine on the flight to Erie, and he would be back at Waterbury-Oxford by 19:00.*

The pilot actually departed Erie at night. There was a fatal crash and the NTSB probable cause states:

> *The loss of partial engine power for undetermined reasons, and the pilot's loss of control after performing an evasive maneuver to avoid trees during a forced landing at night. Factors related to the accident were a rough running engine and the pilots inability to see the trees due to the nighttime conditions. The NTSB accident details are available here.*

While not common, even professionally trained pilots sometimes fail to recognize and respond to hazards and associated risks. An airline accident involving a transport category turbojet taken to its maximum operating altitude resulted in both engines flaming out after an aerodynamic stall. The flight ended in a crash and two fatalities. The NTSB probable cause(s) follows:

> *The National Transportation Safety Board determines the probable cause(s) of this accident to be: (1) the pilots' unprofessional behavior, deviation from standard operating procedures, and poor airmanship, which resulted in an in-flight emergency from which they were unable to recover, in part because of the pilots' inadequate training; (2) the pilots' failure to prepare for an emergency landing in a timely manner, including communicating with air traffic controllers immediately after the emergency about the loss of both engines and the availability of landing sites; and (3)*

the pilots' improper management of the double engine failure checklist, which allowed the engine cores to stop rotating and resulted in the core lock engine condition. Contributing to this accident were (1) the core lock engine condition, which prevented at least one engine from being restarted, and (2) the airplane flight manuals that did not communicate to pilots the importance of maintaining a minimum airspeed to keep the engine cores rotating. The NTSB accident details are available here.

Understanding the Risks Posed by Hazards

A predisposition to respond to persons, situations, or events in a given manner reveals a person's attitude. Studies have identified five hazardous attitudes that can affect a pilot's ability to make sound decisions and exercise authority properly. [*Figure 3-1*]

The Five Hazardous Attitudes
Anti-authority: "Don't tell me." This attitude is found in people who do not like anyone telling them what to do. In a sense, they are saying, "No one can tell me what to do." They may be resentful of having someone tell them what to do or may regard rules, regulations, and procedures as silly or unnecessary. However, it is always pilot prerogative to question authority if it seems to be in error.
Impulsivity: "Do it quickly." This is the attitude of people who frequently feel the need to do something—anything—immediately. They do not stop to think about what they are about to do; they do not select the best alternative; and they do the first thing that comes to mind.
Invulnerability: "It won't happen to me." Many people believe that accidents happen to others, but never to them. They know accidents can happen, and they know that anyone can be affected. They never really feel or believe that they will be personally involved. Pilots who think this way are more likely to take chances and increase risk.
Macho: "I can do it." Pilots who are always trying to prove that they are better than anyone else are thinking, "I can do it, I'll show them." Pilots with this type of attitude will try to prove themselves by taking risks in order to impress others. While this pattern is thought to be a male characteristic, women are equally susceptible.
Resignation: "What's the use?" Pilots who think, "What's the use?" do not see themselves as being able to make a great deal of difference in what happens to them. When things go well, the pilot is apt to think that it is good luck. When things go badly, the pilot may feel that "someone is out to get me," or attribute it to bad luck. The pilot will leave the action to others, for better or worse. Sometimes, such pilots will even go along with unreasonable requests just to be a "nice guy."

Figure 3-1. *Pilots should examine their decisions carefully to ensure that their choices have not been influenced by a hazardous attitude.*

Most pilots sincerely believe that they will respond to hazards appropriately and take actions necessary to avoid accidents. However, a pilot's attitude affects perception of hazards, the analysis of the potential threat, and performance of an appropriate response.

Since attitude influences behavior, pilots should consider their own attitude and the antidote to any hazardous attitude. [*Figure 3-2*] The pilots in the two fatal accidents described above exhibited several of these hazardous attitudes. If they had recognized their attitude toward the hazards and associated risks and considered that their behavior could result in an accident, it is very likely that they would have acted differently (invulnerability). If the general aviation pilot had waited and returned the next day, he might be alive today (impulsivity). The commercial pilots wanted to claim they had flown the aircraft at its maximum altitude (macho). Pilot attitudes regarding hazard analysis clearly play a role in decision-making.

Hazardous Attitude	Antidotes
Macho Steve often brags to his friends about his skills as a pilot and how close to the ground he flies. During a local pleasure flight in his single-engine airplane, he decides to buzz some friends barbecuing at a nearby park.	**Taking chances is foolish.**
Anti-authority Although he knows that flying so low to the ground is prohibited by the regulations, he feels that the regulations are too restrictive in some circumstances.	**Follow the rules. They help prevent accidents.**
Invulnerability Steve is not worried about an accident since he has flown this low many times before, and he has not had any problems.	**It could happen to me.**
Impulsivity As he is buzzing the park, the airplane does not climb as well as Steve had anticipated, and without thinking, he pulls back hard on the yoke. The airspeed drops, and the airplane is close to stalling as the wing brushes a power line.	**Not so fast. Think first.**
Resignation Although Steve manages to recover, the wing sustains minor damage. Steve thinks to himself, "It doesn't really matter how much effort I put in—the end result is the same whether I really try or not."	**I'm not helpless. I can make a difference.**

Figure 3-2. *Antidotes to hazardous attitudes.*

Leading Accident Causes

The aviation accident record has improved considerably in recent years, but the reduction in accident rates has not been uniform across the aviation community. For example, the accident rate for air carriers operating under 14 CFR part 121 was reduced by nearly 80 percent in the ten-year period beginning in the mid-1990s. In contrast, general aviation aircraft operating under 14 CFR part 91 maintained a static accident rate of about one fatal accident per 100,000 flight hours.

The FAA and the general aviation community collaborate through the General Aviation Joint Steering Committee (GAJSC), to suggest safety enhancements that could reduce accidents. As part of this effort, the GAJSC analyzed hundreds of general aviation accidents and evaluated the causal factors. The FAA Fact Sheet on General Aviation Safety ranks the following ten leading causes of general aviation fatal accidents during the period 2001-2016:

1. Loss of control in-flight (LOC-I)
2. Controlled flight into terrain (CFIT)
3. System component failure–powerplant
4. Fuel related
5. Unknown or undetermined
6. System component failure–non powerplant
7. Unintended flight into IMC
8. Midair collisions

9. Low-altitude operations

10. Other

The top four causes of general aviation fatal accidents include loss of control in-flight (LOC-I), controlled flight into terrain (CFIT), system component failure of the powerplant (SCF-PP), and fuel-related issues. These causes often signify the final result of a chain of events. However, an in-depth analysis of these accidents will often reveal inadequate risk management as a common thread. To begin with, pilots should recognize hazards linked to causes of aircraft accidents as presented below:

1. Loss of Control In-flight (LOC-I)–Examples of loss of control scenarios include continued VFR into IMC, wake turbulence upsets, thunderstorm encounters, instrument failure, improper aircraft loading, loss of outside references during flight at night or over water, and conditions that exceed the pilot's capability.

2. Controlled Flight into Terrain (CFIT)–CFIT often results from continued VFR flight into areas with a low ceiling or low visibility, flight at night, incorrect interpretation of a chart, flight at high density altitude, flight in mountainous terrain, or intentionally flying too low.

3. System Component Failure Powerplant (SCF-PP)–This category includes a variety of hazards, some which the pilot or operator may not easily identify. If a pilot experiences difficulty with an engine run-up or experiences an engine issue after maintenance, a significant hazard may exist.

4. Fuel-Related–Pilots still experience fuel starvation or fuel exhaustion. Misunderstanding or mishandling the aircraft's fuel system, a lack of adequate planning, trying to stretch aircraft fuel range, or an unwillingness to take the time or make the effort to stop for fuel contributes to this type of accident.

Identifying Hazards

There are several ways pilots can detect hazards. Pilots should use combinations of methods to detect hazards, including the following:

- Visual Observation–A pilot's observations provide a primary means to identify hazards. For example, a pilot can visually observe thunderstorms and maintain a safe distance from them. A pilot who can see terrain can maneuver to avoid it.

- Preflight Planning–Many hazards can be detected through preflight planning. Weather briefings identify hazards. Aircraft performance calculations, preflight inspections, and other routine procedures may identify hazards.

- On-board Equipment–The availability of lower-cost modern avionics has improved situational awareness in many general aviation aircraft. Technologies such as GPS-based moving map navigation, datalink weather, traffic displays, terrain displays, and synthetic vision help pilots recognize different hazards.

- Radio Communication–Voice radio provides an effective means to find out about hazards. Communication with air traffic controllers and flight service specialists can provide real-time information on weather, air traffic, airspace activity, and other hazards.

- Postflight Inspections–Inspecting the aircraft following the completion of a flight may identify aircraft hazards before the next person flies the aircraft. Common items include condition of tires and brakes, security of access panels and latches, and leaking operating fluids. Properly securing the aircraft may prevent damage, which could affect the next flight.

Using the PAVE Checklist to Identify Hazards

As described in Chapter 1, the PAVE checklist provides a means to identify hazards using four convenient hazard "buckets." Using all four checklist categories before a flight captures most hazards normally encountered. This section discusses hazards associated with each category.

Pilot Hazards

"P" hazards can be classified in terms of both capability and aeromedical factors as follows:

1. Qualification–Does the pilot possess the appropriate pilot certificate, category, class, and type rating needed to operate a specific aircraft under the given set of conditions? Some accidents have occurred when pilots have attempted to operate under IFR without holding an instrument rating. A few accidents occur every year when the pilot did not possess any airman certificate.

2. Currency–Has the pilot logged the minimum number of takeoffs and landings and instrument approaches, flight reviews, or other currency events required by 14 CFR? Are the currency requirements sufficient to guarantee that the pilot will be able to handle the flight requirements?

3. Proficiency–Does the pilot have the ability to manage the conditions expected during flight? For example, suppose a pilot plans an IFR flight with forecast of low ceilings. Under 14 CFR part 61, the pilot needs to have logged six instrument approaches, holding, and tracking within the previous six calendar months to be IFR current. However, if these currency events occurred five months ago, the pilot may lack the proficiency to make the flight safely. If a pilot flies an unfamiliar aircraft, does the pilot have the ability to use the avionics and systems efficiently and properly?

Aeromedical

Aeromedical hazards relate to physical and emotional readiness for flight including:

- Illness–Does a pilot suffer from initial symptoms, ongoing illness, or any aftereffects? Even mild symptoms may be sufficiently debilitating to create a "P" hazard.

- Medication–Could any medications the pilot takes affect the flight? Both prescription and non-prescription over-the-counter (OTC) drugs have side effects that can affect a pilot's physical and mental performance. The FAA provides information regarding OTC drugs here.

- Stress–Has a stressful life situation affected the pilot? Many personal or business events and activities can cause stress. Stress has many manifestations and affects thinking, behavior, and health.

- Alcohol–Has the pilot consumed alcohol recently? The CFRs include a time limit (no consumption within eight hours before a flight), a quantity limit (blood alcohol must be below 0.04 percent), and a performance limit (flight duty prohibited while under the influence of alcohol). Aftereffects of alcohol consumption (dehydration, hangover, and headaches, etc.) may trigger a "P" hazard for longer than eight hours after consumption.

- Fatigue–How alert is the pilot? Fatigue may result from insufficient sleep. However, sufficient sleep only corrects acute fatigue. Chronic fatigue may involve multiple factors and requires additional analysis and remedy. Fatigue can be intensified by hypoxia as well as emotional state. While fatigued pilots have fallen asleep while flying, the effects of fatigue may be subtle. For example, fatigue may degrade cognitive skills and decision-making ability.

- Emotion–Has the pilot experienced an event or received information that creates strong feelings? Emotions may affect normal pilot ability to focus.

The IMSAFE checklist, which is an acronym for Illness, Medication, Stress, Alcohol, Fatigue, and Emotion, can help a pilot identify these hazards. [*Figure 3- 3*] Note that some publications combine Emotion with Stress as the "S" in IMSAFE and leave the "E" to remind pilots about "Eating." Since proper nutrition and hydration affects wellness and safety, a pilot planning a long flight should consider appropriate food and water intake and supply.

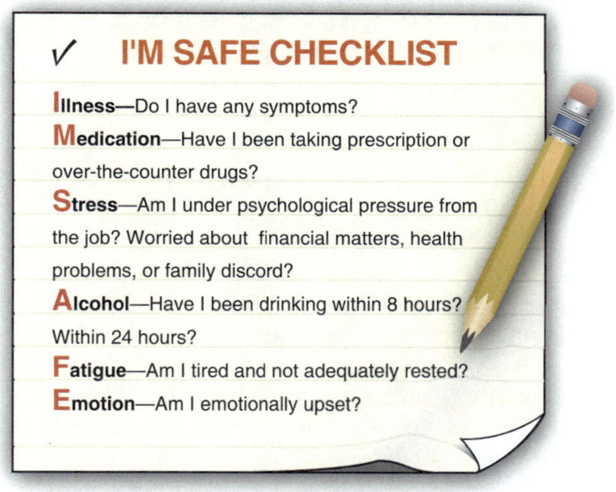

Figure 3-3. *IMSAFE checklist.*

Aircraft Hazards

"A" hazards can be classified in terms of both performance and equipage.

Performance

Aircraft performance hazards may include:

- Fuel and Range–As previously described, fuel issues continue to be a leading cause of general aviation accidents. Planning a flight to the aircraft's maximum range magnifies this "A" hazard. Inaccurate calculations, changing conditions, or the aircraft's failure to achieve "book" speeds and fuel consumption can lead to an incident or accident.

- Takeoff and Landing Performance– Takeoffs and landings become more hazardous when the calculated performance approaches the available runway length.

- Altitude Performance–Operating to or from high altitude airports or cruising at high altitudes may result in a lack of performance. In some cases, this lack of performance may not allow for a safe departure. In situations where a climb could avoid a weather or terrain hazard, the lack of performance might contribute to an incident or accident.

- Payload–Does an aircraft have the capability to carry the passengers, baggage, cargo, and fuel for a planned flight? In addition, operating near maximum takeoff weight reduces climb performance.

- Weight and Balance–Pilots who do not check center of gravity limits may experience difficulty trimming or controlling the aircraft, which could lead to a loss of control in-flight.

Equipage

The avionics and other equipment installed in an aircraft affect both utility and the ease with which a pilot can identify hazards. Equipment considerations include:

- Redundancy–Could equipment failure affect the type of flight contemplated? For example, on a day VFR flight in Class E airspace, having only a single navigation/communication radio is not a major concern. However, for a flight in IMC, having one radio could be considered an "A" hazard. Instrument failure is also a concern in IMC or at night, and backup systems could prevent an accident.

- Autopilot–Operating an aircraft in IMC without an autopilot increases pilot workload. A pilot flying an aircraft in these conditions might consider aircraft without an autopilot an "A" hazard.

- Inoperative Equipment–Inoperative equipment triggers an "A" hazard. For example, an inoperative landing light may make night operation more hazardous, even though a landing light is not required for Part 91 operations when not for hire. A pilot should consider the effect of inoperative equipment in relation to expected flight conditions.

Environmental Hazards

The environment or "V" hazard encompasses weather, terrain, airports, airspace, time of day, and other factors.

Weather

Of all the environmental hazards, weather is the most variable. However, improvements in aviation weather forecasts and improvements in technology make it easier to identify weather hazards.

- Thunderstorms and Convective Activity–Thunderstorms and their associated weather represent a severe hazard to all aviation activities. Severe turbulence, hail, and other phenomena can create the potential for loss of control and may result in structural failure of the aircraft.

- Icing–Icing conditions constitute a hazard, and in-flight ice accretion has resulted in numerous loss of control accidents. Frost, ice, or snow adhering to the aircraft on the ground, if not removed, can also be a hazard.

- Low Ceilings and Visibility–At times, conditions below minimums can extend beyond the range of an IFR flight. Continued VFR flight into IMC continues to cause accidents.

- Turbulence and Winds–Severe turbulence aloft, although not common, can result in loss of control and may lead to aircraft structural failure. Surface winds also constitute a hazard. For example, a crosswind that exceeds an aircraft's demonstrated maximum crosswind component or the pilot's ability may result in loss of control on the ground (LOC-G).

Terrain

Terrain and surface features are a significant hazard to all aircraft. In extreme cold or high pressure, height above ground and obstacles may be less than indicated. Pilots following instrument approach procedures have also been involved in CFIT accidents.

- Mountains, Hills, and Elevated Terrain–Mountainous terrain affects departure, en route, and arrival operations. Numerous airports in the western United States require the use of special procedures.

- Density Altitude–The combination of high temperature and high elevation affects aircraft performance. High density altitude is a "V" hazard that affects takeoffs, climbs, and landings.

- Over-water Operation–Takeoff at night over a large body of water can create a "black hole" effect and require the pilot to immediately shift to control by instruments. Operating over water may not provide a suitable surface for an emergency landing.

Facilities

The departure and arrival facilities pilots use contain various hazards, and these can be aggravated by other environmental factors.

- Airports–Runway dimensions may not be sufficient such that a takeoff or landing can be performed safely under the given conditions.

- Runway Contamination–Wet or snow-covered runways are an environmental hazard. Some airplane flight manuals (AFM) provide little or no guidance on how to modify takeoff and landing distances for contaminated runways.

- Heliports–The aircraft rotor diameter may exceed the space available.

- Seaplane Bases–Conditions that allow for landing may not be sufficient for takeoff. Obstructions may exist below the water and could be affected by tides. Rough water or glassy water conditions may exist.

- Approach Aids and Lighting–A facility without working approach aids and lighting for a given set of operating conditions is a "V" hazard.

Airspace, Air Traffic Control, and Other Aircraft

Airspace requirements and ATC services facilitate safe and efficient operations. However, under some circumstances, their presence or absence constitutes a "V" hazard.

- Prohibited and Restricted Airspace–Different airspace designations and restrictions are meant to protect pilots and aircraft from hazards. For example, entering a prohibited or restricted area without permission can result in conflicts with military aircraft.

- ATC Delays and Service Availability–The ATC system may require route changes or holding, which may require more fuel than expected.

- Air Traffic Density and Collision Hazards–Pilots are responsible for seeing and avoiding other aircraft when flying under VFR or in VMC while flying under IFR. However, under certain conditions, it is difficult to see other aircraft because of haze, sunlight, aircraft position, blind spots, and other factors.

Night Operations

Night operations make it more difficult to see and identify other hazards.

- VFR operations–Visual operations are often hampered by visibility restrictions at night. This restricts a pilot's ability to see and avoid terrain and obstacles, other aircraft, precipitation, and other hazards.

- Single-engine operations–A forced landing at night may require a pilot to deal with unexpected terrain hazards. In addition, the failure of engine accessories, such as an alternator, may lead to total electrical failure.

External Pressure Hazards

External pressures or "E" hazards originate from a variety of personal and business reasons. The pressure to get to a particular destination or to leave at the conclusion of a planned stay can affect a pilot's judgment. Pilots subject to external pressures sometimes fail to consider the other three major categories of hazards.

- Why does the pilot need to fly to a particular destination at a given time? Wanting to be present at a family celebration, wishing to see a terminally ill relative, or the need to be at an important meeting can affect pilot motivation. It may be a simple matter of not wanting to disappoint someone waiting at the destination. It could also include a condition that arises during a flight, such as a sick passenger.

- If a general aviation aircraft is used for business travel, a pilot may experience time pressure after committing to be somewhere at a given time. Business flights place additional pressure on the pilot to conduct the "mission," regardless of the hazards and conditions.

Hazard Combinations

Pilots often need to consider the effect of interactions with several hazards at the same time.

Imagine that a pilot operates from the Elkins-Randolph County airport in Elkins, West Virginia (KEKN). This airport sits in a valley at an elevation of 1,987 feet. The terrain and obstacles on the east and west sides rise to as high as 3,631 feet. The images in *Figure 3-4* and *Figure 3-5* show a photograph and a sectional aeronautical chart excerpt of the Elkins airport.

Figure 3-4. *Elkins, WV airport.*

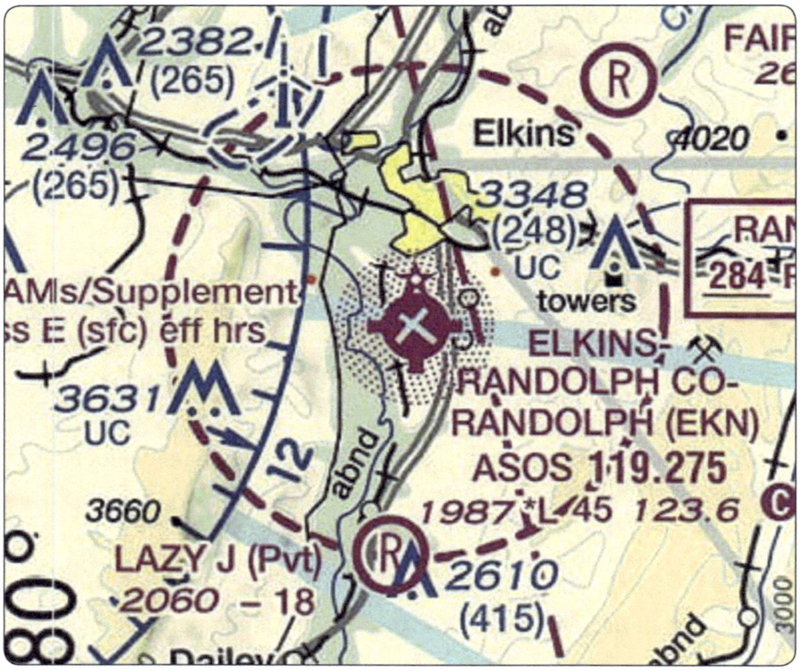

Figure 3-5. *Sectional chart excerpt of Elkins, WV airport.*

The mountains and obstructions on both sides of the Elkins airport are a hazard. However, on a day with good visibility, few clouds, and light winds, the associated risks are low for most aircraft engaged in visual flight rules (VFR) operations.

If the Elkins airport scenario changes to a night operation, the level of risk associated with the combination of hazards increases, and an accident becomes more likely. Pilots exposed to these multiple hazards need to consider the equipment, skill, and experience necessary to operate safely.

Hazards and Associated Risks

While interaction with a hazard can cause an accident, the level of risk associated with the hazard depends on composite of the likelihood for the type of accident and the expected severity of injury as a result of such an accident. Depending on a particular flight mission, each individual risk may be acceptable or unacceptable. In general aviation operations, the tolerance for risk is generally low, and pilots should use risk assessment and management tools to mitigate any unacceptable risk before embarking on a flight.

Using a Flight Risk Assessment Tool (FRAT)

Identifying hazards and associating them with risks can be accomplished using a simple spreadsheet or form during flight planning. The form used to record each hazard is known as a Flight Risk Assessment Tool (FRAT).

Numerical FRATs

A numerical FRAT lists different hazards and an associated number, which indicates the significance of each hazard. The pilot selects the relevant hazards, and derives a total score. Typically, the score falls into three ranges. If the total score is below a certain minimum, the FRAT indicates low risk. If it is in an intermediate range, the pilot is advised to "exercise caution." If the score is above an upper threshold, the FRAT indicates danger. [*Figure 3-6*]

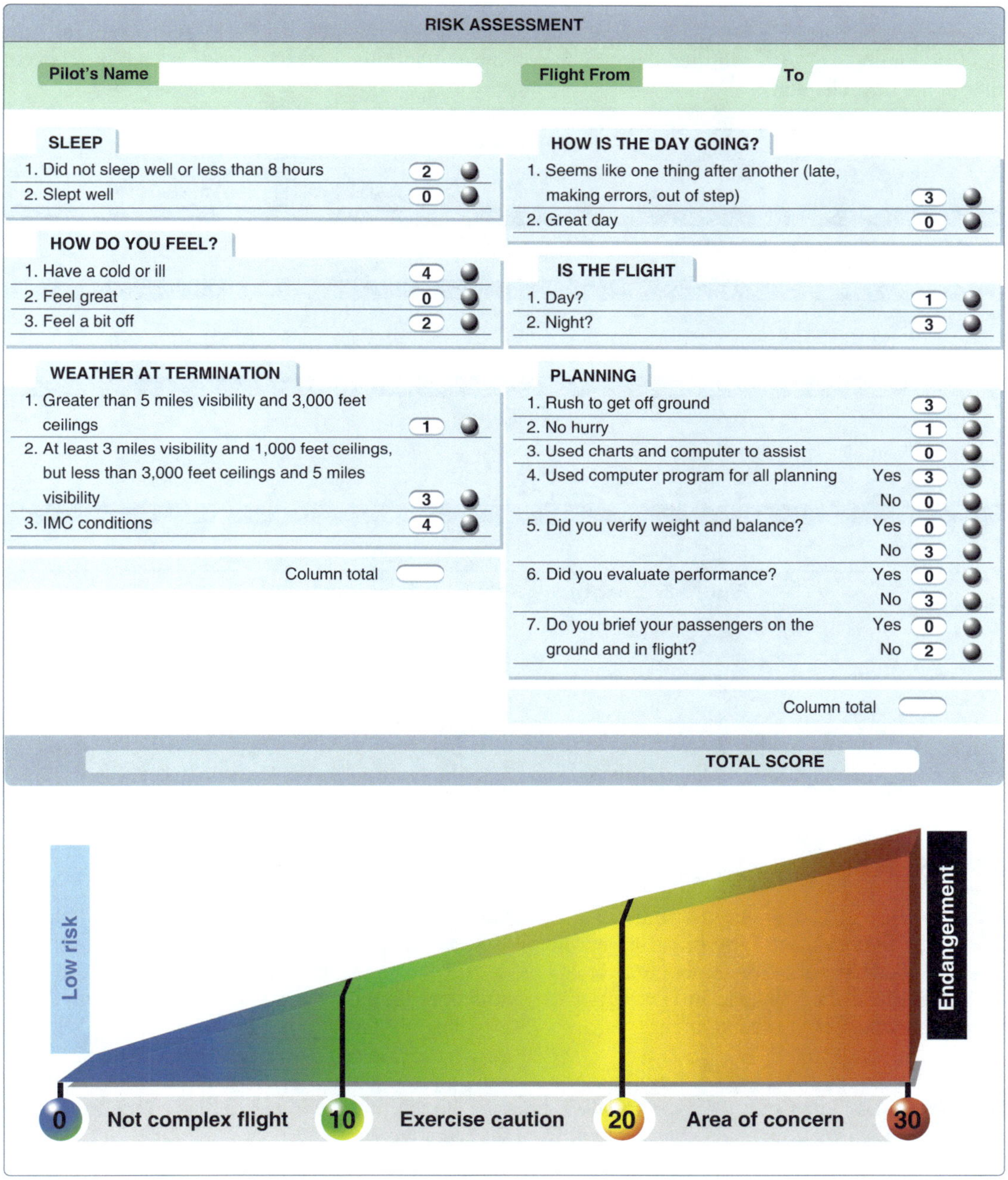

Figure 3-6. *Example of a numerical FRAT.*

The FAA provides a numerical FRAT here. While this type of FRAT is easy to use, it has several drawbacks, including:

1. The form may not cover all the hazards for a particular flight.

2. The range of scores for each risk level may appear arbitrary, leading a pilot to question the results.

3. The form does not encourage the pilot to analyze each hazard. For example, what is the likelihood the condition will lead to an accident and what is the potential accident severity?

4. The form may indicate an overall low level of risk, leading the pilot to ignore the implications of a particular hazard.

Narrative FRATs

This type of FRAT asks the user to identify hazards and associate each hazard with risk. While taking more time to complete, it addresses many of the disadvantages of a numerical FRAT. After identifying the hazards, the process includes a thorough analysis and management of each risk.

The following example of a narrative FRAT has the pilot determine the likelihood and severity for each hazard identified using the PAVE checklist [*Figure 3-6*]. After further analysis, the pilot can determine how to manage each risk. This concept will be explored further in the next chapter.

Flight Risk Assessment Tool

PAVE Area	Hazard	Risk	Likelihood	Severity	Composite Risk	Mitigation Results
Pilot "P"						
Capability						
Aeromedical						
Aircraft "A"						
Fuel/Range/Payload						
Equipment						
Performance						
Environment "V"						
Weather						
Terrain						
Airspace, ATC, Airports						
Night/Over Water						
External Pressure "E"						
Personal						
Business						

Figure 3-7. *Example Flight Risk Assessment Tool.*

Case Study

One way to understand the risk management process is to put it in a real-world context using a case study. The following example will be used in this chapter, as well as Chapters 4 and 5, to illustrate a process to identify hazards, assess the associated risks, and mitigate the risks as needed.

Background and Setting

It is early on Friday, July 1, and Tricia just finished a successful week of consulting for clients in Portland, Boise, Dallas, and Albuquerque. She flew to these locations from her home base in Santa Rosa, California (KSTS) using her single-engine airplane. She had planned to return directly to Santa Rosa, but yesterday evening, her friends from Santa Rosa, Matt and Martha Smith, invited her to spend the weekend in Durango, Colorado where they have a condominium. She gladly accepted their invitation because she would enjoy seeing them.

The flight from Albuquerque to Durango during the day on Friday goes smoothly. Tricia lands at the Animas Air Park (00C), rather than the Durango-La Plata County Airport (KDRO) because the Smith's condo is less than a mile from Animas Air Park, toward town. *Figure 3-8* shows a sectional chart excerpt from the Durango area.

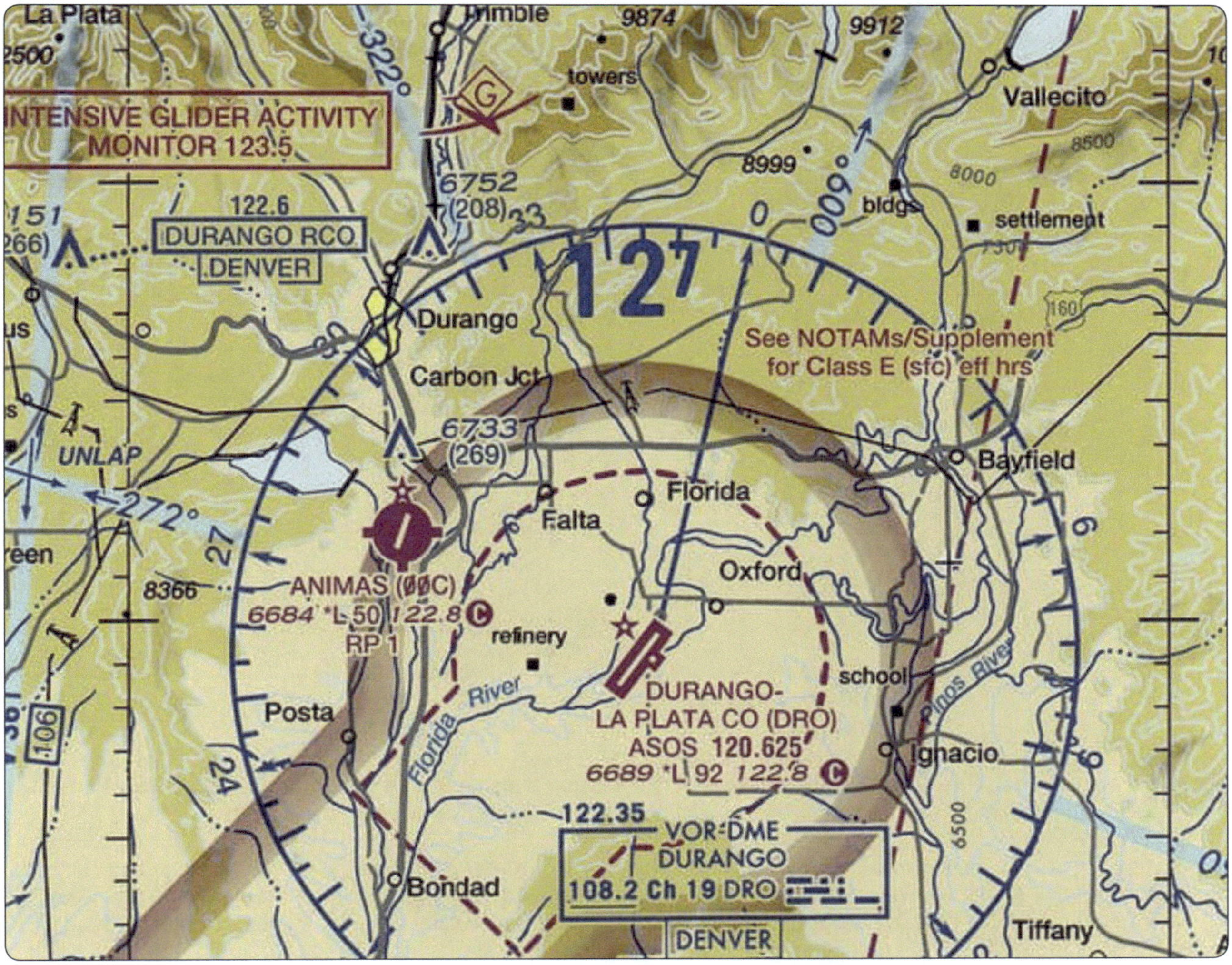

Figure 3-8. *Aeronautical chart excerpt showing Durango, CO.*

Tricia and the Smiths are enjoying the warm-weather weekend with rafting, cycling, and hiking as featured activities. The Smiths are well-established in the Durango social scene, and the three friends go to parties on Friday and Saturday night, with another one scheduled for Sunday night. Finally, on Monday, July 4, there will be a city-sponsored Independence Day celebration where the Smiths will officiate.

It is now late afternoon on Sunday. Tricia and the Smiths are back in their condo relaxing and discussing the weekend. Coincidentally, both Tricia and Martha Smith just received urgent emails from their separate home offices in Santa Rosa, CA, alerting them to critical meetings that are scheduled for Tuesday afternoon–Tricia's at 4 pm and Martha's at 3 pm. Matt tries to book airline tickets from Durango to Santa Rosa for Tuesday morning, and with a worried look, he announces that there are no airline seats available until Wednesday, at the earliest.

Martha Smith then asks Tricia, "Would you be willing to fly us home in your airplane on Tuesday morning? This would allow us all to enjoy the Monday celebration and the party Monday night before taking off early on Tuesday." Tricia replies, "I need to review the weather and do some other planning first, and we can all meet in a couple of hours."

Tricia goes back to her room and begins her analysis. First, she looks at the route that she might take home. Originally, she planned a direct VFR flight back to Santa Rosa, a nonstop flight of 711 nautical miles, as depicted in the sectional chart excerpt in *Figure 3-9*.

Figure 3-9. *The direct route from Durango to Santa Rosa.*

Tricia makes a quick analysis and figures she can fly this trip nonstop in just under five hours, with 6 hours and 45 minutes of endurance with full tanks. She then evaluates the weather and immediately foresees some challenges.

A low-pressure system with a trailing cold front is moving south into northwest Colorado. The front is triggering severe convective activity as it collides with moist air in the southwest. Low ceilings and poor visibility are widespread behind the front, with mountain obscuration and icing in clouds above 8,000 feet. The weather in Durango should remain good VFR on Monday, but change to IMC early Tuesday morning as the weather system slowly moves southeast.

Data

Tricia needs to organize, consider, and evaluate all the information.

Pilot and Passengers

The pilot and passenger data is as follows:

- Current under 14 CFR part 61 for VFR and IFR
- Last instrument time logged four months ago
- Tricia's weight is 130 pounds, the Smiths weigh 340 pounds together
- Tricia has 40 pounds of baggage, the Smiths have 80 pounds

Aircraft

The aircraft data is as follows:

- Not certificated for flight in known icing conditions
- Empty weight: 1903 pounds, Maximum gross weight 2,740 pounds
- Luggage compartment carries 120 pounds
- Current fuel 25 gallons (150 pounds) Fuel capacity 64 gallons (384 pounds)
- Average fuel consumption at 10,000 feet: 8.6 gallons per hour

- Average true airspeed at 10,000 feet: 152 knots
- Calculated takeoff distance at 25° C, 6,700 feet pressure altitude, no wind, and 2,740 pounds: 4,700 feet over a 50-foot obstacle
- Calculated takeoff distance at 25° C, 6,700 feet pressure altitude, no wind, and 2,500 pounds: 3,600 feet over a 50-foot obstacle

Environment

The following is in addition to weather data mentioned earlier:

- Temperatures at Animas Air Park (00C): 25° C mornings, 35° C afternoons, calm winds
- California weather forecast: Good VFR except morning fog on the coast
- Arizona weather forecast: Good VFR weather on Monday, marginal VFR Tuesday

Hazard Identification and Risk Analysis

Tricia decides to begin her risk analysis by identifying the potential hazards and associated risks for the flight to Santa Rosa, using the PAVE checklist. The various hazards and risks may overlap in more than one checklist category, but she wants to identify all the hazards and risks and may consolidate them later in the process.

Pilot

- She is IFR current, but it has been four months since her last proficiency event. This hazard could increase the risk of loss of control in IMC.
- If she consumes alcohol, she needs to allow for a minimum of eight hours prior to the planned departure on Tuesday to be legal. She also needs to be free from any aftereffects from alcohol, which could be magnified by the altitude and result in dehydration. This hazard could increase errors.
- She has been going to bed late and getting up early in Durango. This fatigue hazard could increase the risk of making errors.

Aircraft

- She is concerned about the range/payload trade-off for her airplane. Reducing the range by trading fuel weight for payload could increase the risk of fuel exhaustion.
- Tricia also knows that her aircraft is not approved for flight in known icing conditions and that an icing encounter could lead to loss of control.
- She is concerned about the takeoff from Animas Air Park at gross weight, considering the runway length. This potential hazard could create a risk for an overrun or stall after takeoff. Her personal minimums include a 20 percent additional margin over calculated runway takeoff distance.

Environment

- The weather system moving in from northwest Colorado is the main environmental hazard affecting the flight to Santa Rosa. The presence of both convection and icing could increase the risk of loss of control, or if attempting to stay underneath the clouds in VFR, the risk of CFIT.

- The high, rough terrain in this part of the southwest United States presents a hazard on the route to Santa Rosa. This requires relatively high cruising altitudes which may approach the performance limits of her airplane.

- The departure airport has no ATC services, although fuel is available. ATC may limit the altitude selection en route, which could limit an escape from icing conditions.

External Pressures

- The scheduled meetings back in Santa Rosa on Tuesday generate external pressures. The need to be present in Durango on Monday narrows the departure window to Tuesday morning only. If these pressures are not mitigated, a forced departure on Tuesday morning will mean dealing with the hazards and associated risks related to the pilot, the aircraft, and the environment.

As Tricia tallies up the hazards and associated risks for the planned flight to Santa Rosa, she records them on the FRAT, as shown in *Figure 3-10*. She needs to assess these risks in terms of their likelihood and severity. She strives to complete the risk analysis so she can return and discuss the situation with the Smiths.

Flight Risk Assessment Tool

PAVE AREA	Hazard	Risk	Likelihood	Severity	Composite Risk	Mitigation Results
Pilot "P"						
Capability	Not IFR proficient	LOC				
Aeromedical	Alcohol and lack of sleep	Fatigue related errors				
Aircraft "A"						
Fuel/Range/Payload	Cannot carry full fuel	fuel exhaustion				
Equipment	Not certified for known ice	LOC				
Performance	Marginal takeoff performance	LOC or CFIT				
Environment "V"						
Weather	Thunderstorms, icing low ceilings	LOC and CFIT				
Terrain	High terrain	CFIT				
Airspace, ATC, Airports	Marginal runway length	Overrun				
Night/Over Water	N/A	N/A				
External Pressure "E"						
Personal	N/A	N/A				
Business	Meeting deadlines for myself and Ms. Smith	Increased risk in all other categories				

Figure 3-10. *Case study FRAT with risks identified.*

The risk assessment and mitigation for this case study will continue in Chapters 4 and 5.

Chapter Summary

Poor risk management is a common factor in many general aviation accidents. Pilots can use the PAVE checklist before flight to identify hazards. Pilots can use a FRAT to organize identified hazards and associated risks for additional analysis.

Chapter 4: Assessing Risk

Introduction

Once hazards and their associated risks have been identified, they should be assessed to determine the overall risk level presented by each hazard. This process begins before the flight using the process outlined in the previous chapter. While risk assessment may seem subjective at first, pilots can learn effective risk-management through routine practice and application.

Risk Assessment Components

Risk is the composite of the likelihood (probability) and the severity (consequences) of a particular outcome. Both likelihood and severity can vary in magnitude.

Risk Likelihood

The following terms describe the likelihood of an outcome:

- Probable–An event may occur several times.
- Occasional–An event may occur sometime.
- Remote–An event is unlikely to occur but is possible.
- Improbable–An event is highly unlikely to occur.

To illustrate, consider the likelihood of exceeding airframe structural limits if penetrating a thunderstorm. It is likely that the airframe's structural limits would be exceeded each time this occurs, making the likelihood "probable."

As another example, consider a case where a pilot operates at an airport surrounded by rough terrain. The runways are just long enough to accommodate the aircraft. The possibility exists for a runway overrun on each landing. Given this data, an overrun could occur sometime, and the likelihood is "occasional."

Risk Severity

The following terms describe the severity of an outcome.

- Catastrophic–Results in fatalities and/or total airframe loss.
- Critical–Severe injury or major airframe or property damage.
- Marginal–Minor injury or minor airframe or property damage.
- Negligible–Less than minor injury or damage.

To illustrate, consider the example of penetrating a thunderstorm. A loss of control event exceeding airframe structural limits could result in either severe injuries or fatalities and airframe loss, creating either a "critical" or a "catastrophic" outcome.

In the example of the marginal runway length, an overrun could cause major damage to the aircraft and possible severe injuries, or a "critical" outcome.

Using a Risk Assessment Matrix

Once risk likelihood and severity have been determined, the pilot may use a tabular matrix to find the composite of these two parameters. [*Figure 4-1*]

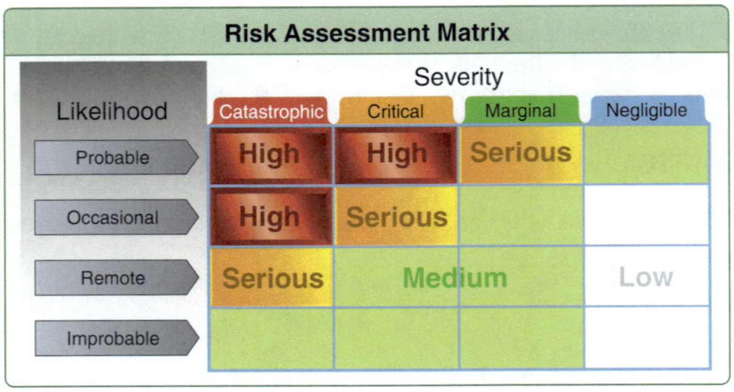

Figure 4-1. *Risk Assessment Matrix.*

Cross-matching the likelihood and severity on the matrix determines the composite risk. A thunderstorm penetration, with "catastrophic" severity and either "probable" or "occasional" likelihood, constitutes a high (red) risk level. The runway overrun, with "critical" severity and "occasional" likelihood, constitutes a serious (yellow) risk level.

The medium (green) risk level implies a "go" decision for a planned or ongoing flight. However, in this case, risk should still be mitigated if possible.

The high (red) or serious (yellow) categories imply "no-go" unless the pilot finds a means to reduce the risk, such that the next iteration of risk assessment indicates a medium or low risk.

Risk analysis should begin hours, days, or even weeks before a flight. For a simple flight, hours in advance may suffice. However, for a complex flight with multiple legs or a series of flights over several days, a pilot should begin to consider hazards and associated risks over an extended time period.

Matrix Errors

When assigning a risk level to a hazard using a matrix, the results could be subject to certain errors.

Accuracy

The matrix provides discrete results that depend on the accurate assignment of likelihood and severity. While conducting a risk assessment, a pilot may be unsure of the likelihood or severity for a particular risk or find it difficult to choose between adjacent parameters. In such cases, pilots should apply the more conservative parameter(s), which place the risk at a higher level. Pilots learning risk analysis should seek the opinion of a more experienced pilot or an instructor if there is any doubt as to the accuracy of inputs.

Skewing

Pilots sometimes use inputs that skew the risk toward a lower level due to the desire to complete a flight.

Obsolescence

The matrix results lose relevance if the hazards change before a flight departs. Pilots should verify and reevaluate their risk assessment based on current information and conditions before flight.

Case Study

Note: Refer to the case study section of Chapter 3 if needed.

Risk Assessment Analysis

The pilot, Tricia, identified nine separate hazards and associated risks that will affect a direct non-stop flight from Animas Air Park (00C) in Colorado to the Santa Rosa, California airport (KSTS). Now, she begins the process of assessing these risks using PAVE checklist elements.

Pilot

Tricia identified both capability and aeromedical risks. She concludes that reduced IFR proficiency means that a loss of control in-flight (LOC-I) event is possible although unlikely. A LOC-I event, especially in convection or icing conditions, could result in a fatal accident. A combination of "remote" likelihood and "catastrophic" severity indicates a serious (yellow) risk on the risk assessment matrix.

She also self-assessed her aeromedical risks using the IMSAFE checklist and identified alcohol and fatigue as potential hazards. The risks associated with these hazards could lead to multiple in-flight errors that could result in major damage or injury. Collectively, she assesses these risks as having "occasional" likelihood and "critical" severity. On the risk assessment matrix, this combination indicates a serious (yellow) risk. [*Figure 4-2*]

Flight Risk Assessment Tool

PAVE Area	Hazard	Risk	Likelihood	Severity	Composite Risk	Mitigation Results
Pilot "P"						
Capability	Not IFR proficient	LOC	remote	catastrophic	serious	
Aeromedical	Alcohol and lack of sleep	Fatigue related errors	occasional	critical	serious	

Figure 4-2. *FRAT excerpt for pilot hazards and associated risks.*

Aircraft

She identified three areas that pertain to aircraft-related risk. During a non-stop flight, the likelihood of fuel exhaustion increases if extensive deviation around weather is needed. Fuel exhaustion over rugged western terrain could result in a fatal accident. Her assessment results in a "remote" likelihood with "catastrophic" consequences, which indicate a serious (yellow) risk on the risk assessment matrix.

Tricia also noted that her aircraft is not approved for flight in known icing conditions and that a flight along the planned route might encounter icing conditions at some point. Even with an "occasional" likelihood, this could generate a CFIT or LOC-I event with fatalities, or "catastrophic" consequences, thus indicating a high (red) risk on the risk assessment matrix.

Finally, the aircraft may lack the performance needed to depart from the 5,000-foot runway at Animas Air Park. Having the Smiths on board, everyone's baggage, and a reduced fuel load would result in a takeoff at the aircraft's maximum gross weight of 2,740 pounds. The calculated takeoff distance would be 4,700 feet, and using her 20 percent safety factor produces a desired runway length of 5,640 feet, which exceeds the available runway distance. Under these conditions, Tricia determines that an overrun is possible at least some of the time and could cause major damage or severe injuries. This "occasional" likelihood and "critical" severity produces a serious (yellow) risk level from the risk assessment matrix. [*Figure 4-3*]

Flight Risk Assessment Tool

PAVE Area	Hazard	Risk	Likelihood	Severity	Composite Risk	Mitigation Results
Aircraft "A"						
Fuel/Range/Payload	Cannot carry full fuel	Fuel exhaustion	remote	catastrophic	serious	
Equipment	Not certified for known ice	LOC	occasional	catastrophic	high	
Performance	Marginal takeoff performance	Overrun, LOC, or CFIT	occasional	critical	serious	

Figure 4-3. *FRAT excerpt for aircraft hazards and associated risks.*

Environment

She identified three areas with environment-related risk. The weather hazards on the direct route to Santa Rosa include thunderstorms, icing, and low ceilings. There could be severe turbulence in the convective activity, which covers most of the route and poses at least an upset potential at some time, producing an "occasional" likelihood. An upset in severe turbulence could result in a LOC-I event and "catastrophic" fatal accident. The "occasional" likelihood and "catastrophic" severity indicate a high (red) risk on the risk assessment matrix.

Tricia's original proposed route traverses some very high and rugged terrain. If she were to attempt to fly under the low ceilings and weather, the terrain would be a hazard with an associated CFIT risk. A CFIT event, while unlikely for a pilot with her experience, would still be possible and could result in fatalities. This "remote" likelihood and "catastrophic" severity indicate a serious (yellow) risk on the risk assessment matrix.

The Animas Air Park elevation of 6,684 feet combined with July temperatures result in a high density altitude, which constitutes a hazard. The combination of high density altitude and high terrain in the area could lead to a "catastrophic" CFIT accident. This could occur at least sometime or with "occasional" likelihood. The combination of "occasional" likelihood and "catastrophic" severity indicate a high (red) risk on the risk assessment matrix.

Flight Risk Assessment Tool

PAVE Area	Hazard	Risk	Likelihood	Severity	Composite Risk	Mitigation Results
Environment "V"						
Weather	Thunderstorms, icing, low ceilings	LOC and CFIT	occasional	catastrophic	high	
Terrain	High terrain	CFIT	occasional	catastrophic	high	
Airspace, ATC, Airports	High density altitude	CFIT	occasional	catastrophic	high	
Night/Over Water	N/A	N/A				

Figure 4-4. *FRAT excerpt for environment hazards and associated risks.*

Both Tricia and Martha face pop-up business events that appear to be critical, and Tricia has agreed to provide a solution to their transportation requirement.

Tricia feels the pressure to get to Santa Rosa before the Tuesday meeting. The Smiths are good friends, and she does not want to disappoint them. She feels additional pressure because the Smiths are expected to officiate at the Independence Day festivities and wish to attend parties that night. They may not be aware of any reason why Tricia could not depart early on Tuesday and get to Santa Rosa in time for their meetings using a single-engine GA airplane.

She concludes that external pressures are magnifying the identified risks, indicating a "probable" likelihood and "catastrophic" severity with high (red) risk levels.

Flight Risk Assessment Tool

PAVE Area	Hazard	Risk	Likelihood	Severity	Composite Risk	Mitigation Results
External Pressure "E"						
Personal	N/A	N/A				
Business	Meeting deadlines for myself and Ms. Smith	Increased risk in all other categories	probable	catastrophic	high	

Figure 4-5. *FRAT Excerpt for external pressure hazards and associated risks.*

She finishes recording her risk assessment analysis [*Figure 4-6*] and begins determining ways to mitigate the risks (see the case study section in Chapter 5, Mitigating Risk). She will soon need to discuss the next steps with the Smiths.

Flight Risk Assessment Tool						
PAVE Area	**Hazard**	**Risk**	**Likelihood**	**Severity**	**Composite Risk**	**Mitigation Results**
Pilot "P"						
Capability	Not IFR proficient	LOC	remote	catastrophic	serious	
Aeromedical	Alcohol and lack of sleep	Fatigue related errors	occasional	critical	serious	
Aircraft "A"						
Fuel/Range/Payload	Cannot carry full fuel	Fuel exhaustion	remote	catastrophic	serious	
Equipment	Not certified for known ice	LOC	occasional	catastrophic	high	
Performance	Marginal takeoff performance	Overrun, LOC, or CFIT	occasional	critical	serious	
Environment "V"						
Weather	Thunderstorms, icing, low ceilings	LOC and CFIT	occasional	catastrophic	high	
Terrain	High terrain	CFIT	occasional	catastrophic	high	
Airspace, ATC, Airports	High density altitude	CFIT	occasional	catastrophic	high	
Night/Over Water	N/A	N/A				
External Pressure "E"						
Personal	N/A	N/A				
Business	Meeting deadlines for myself and Ms. Smith	Increased risk in all other categories	probable	catastrophic	high	

Figure 4-6. *FRAT hazards and associated risks.*

Chapter Summary

Risk assessment is a critical element in the risk analysis process. To determine overall risk levels, the pilot assesses both risk likelihood and risk severity for all identified hazards. The primary tools for this process are the FRAT and the risk assessment matrix. A pilot's risk assessment accuracy should improve with practice.

Chapter 5: Mitigating Risk

Introduction

Risk mitigation reduces the likelihood or predicted severity of potential effects of hazards. As discussed in Chapter 4, Assessing Risk, high (red) and serious (yellow) risks should be mitigated. High risks the pilot cannot mitigate should lead to a no-go decision. Departing with serious risks is also an abnormal situation that calls for additional mitigation. The risk mitigation process may start days or weeks before a flight and depends on the complexity of the plan.

Air carrier, charter, and fractional operations conducted under 14 CFR parts 121, 135, and 91 Subpart K normally preclude operations in the serious and high-risk categories. Corporate turbojet operators also typically adhere to this standard. In addition to regulatory requirements, these operators utilize concepts, procedures, and tools such as safety management systems (SMS) to ensure risks are identified, assessed, and managed appropriately. General aviation pilots can manage risk in a professional manner as well. Risks should be managed such that they are mitigated to medium (green) levels or lower.

Risk mitigation may also allow a pilot to undertake or complete a flight that would otherwise be subject to unacceptable risks. Conversely, the pilot should not depart if the same process reveals safe flight is not possible under the given conditions.

If having a doubt about risk mitigation, a pilot should consider the value of mitigation against the potential cost of property damage and loss of life. A saying goes, safety costs a lot less than an accident. In fact, risk mitigation makes long-term economic sense.

Preflight Risk Mitigation Strategies

Pilots choose from a variety of strategies to mitigate risks, and different strategies may apply to different hazards. Nevertheless, there are a few general strategies that are effective for each area on the PAVE checklist. Pilot, aircraft, and external pressure risks respond well to early, direct action. On the other hand, the scope of many environmental hazards often favors avoidance as a mitigation strategy.

Mitigating Pilot Risks

Personal minimums that account for pilot experience and proficiency mitigate some risks. Pilots flying unfamiliar aircraft may need to raise their personal minimums for that aircraft. When training, pilots can take advantage of scenarios that include risk management in addition to pilot skill elements. Self-evaluation after a flight may alert a pilot of the need for additional training, which may also decrease future risk. If there is any doubt concerning the outcome of a flight, the pilot should consider hiring an instructor or a mentor pilot and making the trip a learning experience.

Use of and careful consideration of the IMSAFE checklist (illness, medication, stress, alcohol, fatigue, emotion) reduces aeromedical risk.

Mitigating Aircraft Risks

Factoring performance data to create safety margins mitigates some risks. Using an aircraft with redundant systems or an aircraft with automation that reduces pilot workload also lowers accident risk. Additionally, addressing discrepancies and conducting proper maintenance can increase reliability and reduce risk. Thorough preflight and postflight inspections also mitigate aircraft risks.

Carrying enough fuel with a sufficient reserve reduces the likelihood of a low-fuel emergency or a forced landing. On some flights, planning for a fuel stop reduces that risk.

If the pilot has a choice, the selection of aircraft may reduce risk. The decision may consider the aircraft performance, the number of engines, known icing capability, and avionics or automation available.

Mitigating Environmental Risks

Flight in the proximity of some environmental hazards may lead to serious or catastrophic accidents. Avoidance strategies reduce the risk by lowering the accident likelihood. This requires pilots to plan, exercise patience, remain flexible, and be creative.

Circumnavigate the Hazard

For some hazards, such as convective activity and very high terrain, a possible mitigation may be a plan to circumnavigate the hazard.

Go Above or Below the Hazard

Sometimes a plan to fly at a different altitude reduces accident likelihood. Pilots can plan for altitudes that keep the aircraft above or below icing conditions. Many instrument pilots who operate aircraft that are not approved for flight in known icing conditions apply personal minimums to avoid conditions below certain temperatures or where the freezing level is at or below the minimum en-route altitude.

Change Departure Time or Date

Advancing or delaying a departure may reduce risk likelihood. For example, on a day when a line of afternoon thunderstorms is forecast, a pilot could plan for an early morning departure or wait until the thunderstorms dissipate and depart late in the afternoon. For some meteorological hazards, such as an incoming low-pressure system, the pilot might choose to depart the day before originally planned.

Cancel the Flight

Canceling a flight is necessary if the pilot cannot mitigate risk sufficiently by other means. The cancellation option is easier if another means of transportation is available or if long-term rescheduling is an option.

Mitigating External Pressure Risks

External pressures can be either subtle or overt. Because it may involve passengers or others waiting for the arrival, it is best to inform them of the need for flexibility.

Local Versus Transportation Flights

A local pleasure flight can still be subject to external pressures, but it is easier to cancel than a scheduled flight related to transportation to an event. When planning a local flight with friends, for example, the pilot can reduce external pressures by telling them in advance that the flight could be canceled at the last minute due to weather or other reasons. For an IFR transportation flight, persons meeting the flight can use an application to know if the flight will arrive as planned. For a VFR flight anyone meeting the flight may wait at home and get notified after the flight arrives.

Personal Versus Business Flights

Pilots who fly business associates may feel significant external pressures. The pilot should manage passenger expectations and may plan for alternative travel options as a means to reduce risk.

Case Study

Note: Refer to the case study supporting data in Chapter 3, Identifying Hazards and Associated Risks, and the risk assessment matrix in Chapter 4, Assessing Risk, to continue the risk mitigation phase of the case study.

Risk Mitigation Analysis

Tricia diligently identified the hazards and assessed the risks of her proposed flight from Durango, CO to Santa Rosa, CA. She should now mitigate the high and serious risks that she identified during the assessment phase. She identified four high and five serious risks that she should attempt to mitigate by reducing risk likelihood, severity, or both.

Tricia starts by reconsidering the overall plan for this flight. She rules out making a non-stop flight because carrying the Smiths and their baggage would require a reduced fuel load, which in this case is a serious (yellow) risk. In addition, the direct route could lead to encounters with thunderstorms, icing conditions, areas of low ceilings, and high terrain. Furthermore, she realizes they should leave Monday morning, rather than Tuesday, because of the incoming front and low-pressure area. She also notes that there may be an issue with fog and low ceilings at Santa Rosa due to the coastal marine layer. This may dissipate by noon, but it is not yet possible to predict.

Tricia starts by calculating the allowable fuel load. With an empty weight of 1,903 pounds and a maximum allowable gross weight of 2,740 pounds, the useful load works out to 837 pounds. Tricia weighs 130 pounds, the Smiths together weigh 340 pounds. Together Tricia and the Smiths have 120 pounds of baggage. Tricia also has an electronic flight bag (EFB) and pilot gear totaling seven pounds. This leaves 240 pounds for fuel, which is 40 gallons. The airplane currently has 25 gallons on board.

There is a serious (yellow) hazard if making a gross weight takeoff from the Animas Air Park (00C). She decides to ask the Smiths to take a taxi to the Durango – La Plata County Airport (KDRO), which is about a ten-mile ride for them and a 7-nautical mile flight for her. It has a 9,200-foot runway. She can add 18 gallons of fuel before the short flight to Durango – La Plata County Airport, and can depart from there at gross weight, which includes 40 gallons of fuel. She plans to make one additional fuel stop.

After a thorough analysis and weather briefing, she elects to fly a southern route to avoid hazardous weather. She plans to refuel at the Barstow-Daggett, CA airport (KDAG). The 490 NM route from Durango – La Plata County Airport uses the Winslow, AZ (INW) VOR as a waypoint and should take 3 hours and 15 minutes. She will have 4 hours and 30 minutes endurance. From there, she will fly to Santa Rosa using the Palmdale, CA (PMD) VOR as a waypoint. This route is 390 NM and should take 2 hours 45 minutes with a 4 hour and 30 minute endurance. [*Figure 5-1*]

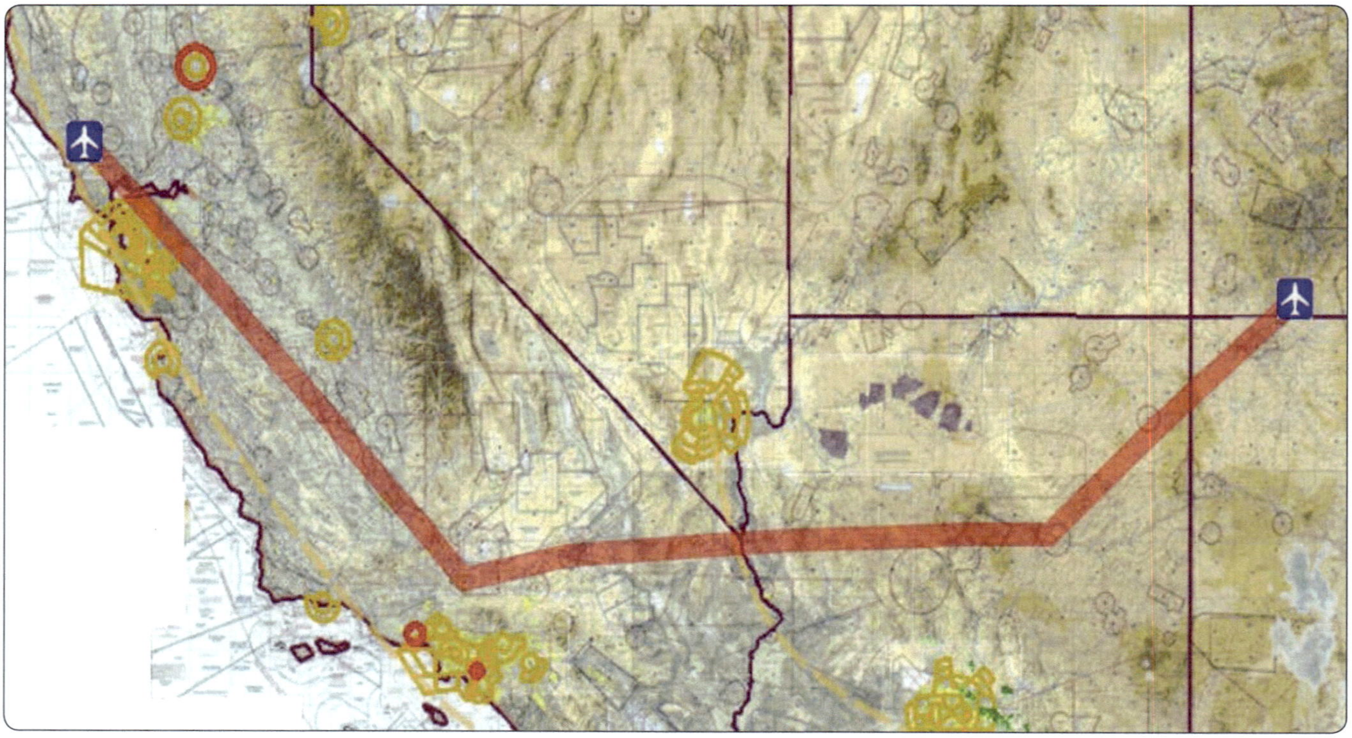

Figure 5-1. *Modified route.*

The total distance along this route is 880 NM, versus the straight-line distance of 711 NM. The additional 169 NM adds about 1 hour and 15 minutes to the total flight time.

She mitigated the aircraft and environmental risks using this plan. She should also deal with the external pressure risks associated with leaving a day early, given the need for the Smiths to forgo the Monday festivities in Durango. An early departure also reduces the external pressures associated with making the Tuesday afternoon meetings on time. Tricia needs to explain the risk analysis to the Smiths and show them why a Monday departure is necessary.

She has concerns related to her instrument proficiency. To compensate, she decides to add 500 feet to her personal minimums for an instrument approach into Santa Rosa. This might require landing at a suitable alternate airport. With the predicted fuel load, she calculates that Sacramento Executive Airport (KSAC), 62 NM from KSTS and well inland, would be a good alternate.

She also considers pilot aeromedical risks. She will consume no alcohol, have an early dinner, and go to bed early. She also increases her intake of water. These actions should help avoid dehydration.

Having addressed all the previously identified risks, she completes the FRAT for the proposed trip, listing all of her mitigations. The completed FRAT in *Figure 5-2* shows all the risks mitigated to medium or low levels. For illustrative purposes, the recalculated risk levels are shown on one sheet showing the before and after. When the conditions change significantly, such as for rescheduling or a change of aircraft, the pilot would normally redo the risk analysis using a fresh worksheet.

Flight Risk Assessment Tool

PAVE Area	Hazard	Risk	Likelihood	Severity	Composite Risk	Mitigation Results
Pilot "P"						
Capability	Not IFR proficient	LOC	remote	catastrophic	serious	Add 500' to minimums improbable/catastrophic now medium
Aeromedical	Alcohol and lack of sleep	Fatigue related errors	occasional	critical	serious	No alcohol/adequate rest remote/marginal now medium
Aircraft "A"						
Fuel/Range/Payload	Cannot carry full fuel	Fuel exhaustion	remote	catastrophic	serious	Add fuel stop improbable/negligible now low
Equipment	Not certified for known ice	LOC	occasional	catastrophic	high	Avoid icing conditions remote/marginal now medium
Performance	Marginal takeoff performance	Overrun, LOC, or CFIT	occasional	critical	serious	Depart from KDRO remote/marginal now medium
Environment "V"						
Weather	Thunderstorms, icing, low ceilings	LOC and CFIT	occasional	catastrophic	high	Fly well south of front remote/critical now medium
Terrain	High terrain	CFIT	occasional	catastrophic	high	Deviate south improbable/critical now medium
Airspace, ATC, Airports	High density altitude	CFIT	occasional	catastrophic	high	Depart from KDRO remote/marginal now medium
External Pressure "E"						
Personal & Business	Meeting deadlines for myself and Ms. Smith	Increased risk in all other categories	probable	catastrophic	high	Brief Smiths, depart Monday AM, shuttle Smiths to KDRO, Add fuel stop improbable/negligible now low

Figure 5-2. *Case study FRAT with risks mitigated.*

Of the nine risks assessed, she originally assessed four as high (red) and five as serious (yellow). According to her analysis and mitigations, the risk for the current plan has seven medium (green) and two low (white) risks.

Tricia meets with the Smiths. They agree with the early departure from Durango and the other mitigations. Matt Smith makes a few phone calls and returns with word that all of Monday's festivities will go forward, but without the Smiths in attendance.

This risk mitigations used for the flight include the following:

1. Adding a safety margin to personal minimums for instrument approaches;
2. Abstaining from alcohol consumption, eating properly, and getting sufficient sleep;
3. Reducing the departure fuel load and adding a fuel stop;
4. Rescheduling to depart a day early;
5. Departing with passengers from the Durango – La Plata County Airport, rather than from Animas Air Park; and
6. Flying along a more southerly route to avoid weather hazards.

While on the ground in Daggett, CA for the planned fuel stop, Tricia checks the weather, which shows that the fog and low ceilings are persisting at Santa Rosa. She understands the potential consequences of slightly elevated risk if making an ILS approach with a 200- to 300-foot ceiling, and confirms her risk analysis remains valid by noting that her alternate, Sacramento Executive Airport, is reporting clear skies as forecast. She prepares her EFB for the possible diversion to Sacramento and reviews the airport information. This preparation alleviates the stress she may feel about diverting. She relieves external pressures by discussing a potential diversion with the Smiths, who indicate they will accept whatever decision she makes.

Within an hour after departure, the fog at Santa Rosa has lifted, and she executes a routine landing.

Several days later, Tricia receives a complementary note from the Smiths praising her consideration for safety.

Balanced Approach to Risk Management

The hypothetical case study used in Chapters 3 through 5 represents a moderately complex scenario covering the flight of a general aviation aircraft on a transportation flight.

It is appropriate to conduct a full risk management process for any flight, including the use of a FRAT. However, for less complex flights, such as a flight in the vicinity of the airport on a sunny day with no wind, the completion of a FRAT may not be necessary.

To enhance risk management accuracy and skill, consider the following steps:

- Take risk management and SRM courses.
- Obtain risk management training from a flight or ground instructor.

- Use a formal risk management process to reduce risk on all complex flights.
- If not using a FRAT, continue to use the PAVE checklist to identify hazards and assess and mitigate the associated risks.

Chapter Summary

Risk mitigation identifies hazards and reduces the likelihood or potential severity of associated risks. It may allow a pilot to undertake a flight that would otherwise generate unacceptable risk. In other cases, the risk mitigation process may identify high and serious risks that cannot be mitigated, which may require rescheduling, cancellation, or alternate transportation. A FRAT can enhance any risk mitigation analysis, but may not be required for simpler flights, provided the pilot has sufficient risk management skill. A brief FAA Safety Team (FAASTeam) video on risk-based decision-making summarizes many concepts discussed in this chapter.

Chapter 6: Threat and Error Management

Introduction

Pilots use risk management as described in earlier chapters to analyze the likelihood and potential severity of an incident or accident based on identified hazards. The process takes time, thought, and collection of information pertinent to the flight. However, once a planned operation begins, a pilot may encounter unforeseen hazards or threats. In addition, a pilot may respond inappropriately to a given condition, thus making an error. This chapter provides strategies pilots may use once flight begins.

Threats

Threats have the following characteristics:

- Threats occur outside the influence of the flight crew; they are not controlled by the pilot.
- Threats increase the operational complexity of a flight.
- Threats may appear suddenly, and may limit the time available for analysis.
- A threat requires effective management to contain risk within acceptable levels.

Some common threats include:

- Malfunction of aircraft systems, engines, flight controls, or automation.
- Various unforecast weather hazards.
- Collision hazards, including wildlife on airports and birds in the air.
- Unexpected sudden reductions in visibility.
- Closures of facilities, runways, or taxiways while en route.
- Unreported poor braking action or surface contamination.
- Malfunction of a radio navigation aid or service after takeoff.
- Unexpected ATC clearances, restrictions, or reroutes that may significantly increase workload.
- Controller errors, radio congestion, or communication failure.
- Cabin events.
- Undetected improper refueling or fuel contamination.

What is an Error?

Errors are deviations from intended or expected actions and result in a reduction in safety margins. They include both unintentional and intentional acts. They do not require the presence of a threat and can occur spontaneously. Errors may cause confusion and increase workload.

Causes of Errors

Errors may result from insufficient training and experience, inadequate flight planning or preparation, external pressures, and physiological and psychological effects.

Insufficient Training & Experience

A pilot who lacks training or experience regarding a given set of conditions may not be in a position to respond appropriately to a related sequence of events and the potential for an inappropriate decision or error increases. Organizations often provide training and supervised operating experience for this reason. General aviation pilots who are enthusiastic about meeting new challenges may find themselves in an unfamiliar situation that may result in serious errors. Pilots seeking the thrill of an adventure should consider the potential danger from errors that may occur.

Inadequate Flight Planning or Preparation

Chapters 3, 4, and 5 of this handbook discuss risk analysis as an important step in the flight planning process. However, the pilot can only conduct a preflight risk analysis based on the information gathered before flight. Inadequate flight planning may leave a pilot in unanticipated conditions and can lead to errors. For example, a pilot dropped off a passenger at the Edward F. Knapp State airport (KMPV) in rural Vermont and expected to refuel for the return trip to White Plains, New York (KHPN). Upon arrival, fuel or other services were not available since it was the weekend. The pilot thought about waiting but decided to fly home after estimating the fuel would be sufficient. The pilot filed a flight plan in the air as visibility started to diminish after departure. Soon after, ATC required a hold as the destination airport had closed for snow removal. The entire region was becoming affected by a snowstorm, and the pilot was running low on fuel. Luckily, after explaining the situation to the controller, the pilot was able to divert to Bridgeport in Connecticut (KBDR), which was the last airport open in the area. Fortunately, the ceiling was just above minimums for the instrument approach, and the pilot was able to land the aircraft in a few inches of snow. Bridgeport closed shortly thereafter for snow removal.

Physiological Effects

Some of the items listed on the I'm Safe checklist (illness, medication, stress, alcohol, fatigue) have the potential to cause pilot errors. For example, it may become difficult or impossible for a stressed or fatigued pilot to focus on a situation or task. Not acting when necessary also constitutes an error.

Limitations affect human senses and perception. For example, when will a pilot see another aircraft on a collision course? The avoidance maneuver may depend not only on where the pilot is looking, but also on the pilot's individual sense of vision combined with all the visual signals received at the same time.

Psychological Effects

Psychological effects include stress, emotion, expectation bias, and the effects of personality.

Stress & Emotion

While pilots should self-evaluate for stress and emotion during preflight mitigation analysis, stress and emotion do sometimes affect a flight in progress. External pressures from outside sources including supervisors, family, and friends may bias a pilot to make an error in an effort to complete a flight as originally planned. What does the pilot actually think about before making a decision? Does the desire to complete a flight as planned influence or outweigh the need to reduce risk? Only the pilot knows the thought process that leads to a decision, but making safety other than the top priority may cause the pilot to err.

An emotional response could appear spontaneously and lead to an error at any time. After an emotional shock or an important life event, the pilot may not be able to concentrate on the current conditions. On the other hand, individuals may become relaxed during flight and may not be sufficiently alert to react to a threat or error. Occasionally, pilots overfly their destination because they have become completely relaxed. If here today, Aristotle would say that errors become more likely if the pilot is obsessed to the point of exclusion of all else or if the pilot is generally disinterested in the events at hand. Appropriate focus and concentration are the golden mean.

Expectation Bias

A pilot's erroneous assessment may persist even though it is wrong and despite available evidence to indicate the error. The term for this phenomenon is expectation bias. The NTSB has investigated numerous accidents and incidents that involved pilot errors resulting from expectation bias, particularly in night VMC when fewer cues aid in airport and runway identification. For example, in January 2014, a Boeing 737 landed at the wrong airport in Branson, Missouri, in night VMC. The flight crew expected that the visually identified airport and runway were the intended destination and did not reference flight deck displays to verify the airport and runway. As a result, the airplane landed on Runway 12 at M. Graham Clark Downtown Airport instead of Runway 14 at Branson Airport.

A general aviation pilot routinely flew to a specific airport with parallel runways. The airport had one runway closed by NOTAM for several months, but after some time, the runway closure was reversed. The NOTAM was no longer for 19R/1L, but for 19L/1R. Even after reading the NOTAM and listening to the ATIS broadcast, the pilot perceived it as it had been previously. An error occurred when the pilot initiated an approach to the closed runway.

When presented with conflicting information, some pilots will try to suppress that information if it does not fit in with the expectation rather than triggering an internal "uh-oh." The phenomenon, not to be confused with expectation bias, has the slightly different name "confirmation bias." The result of either, if uncorrected, may lead to an error. Either case results in the pilot continuing with a plan despite clues indicating the situation is not as perceived. Fatigue tends to stop pilots from taking extra steps to verify perceived reality and contributes to expectation and confirmation bias susceptibility.

An incident at the San Francisco, California airport (KSFO) is another example involving expectation bias. The NTSB docket for this incident provides extensive information regarding expectation bias and is available here.

Expectation bias often occurs on the ground while taxiing. Pilots may expect a particular taxi route and perceive the clearance as expected rather than as given by ATC. Pilots familiar with a particular airport who routinely receive the same taxi clearance may be more susceptible to this error.

Pilots are often thought of as being calm and rational. Like all people, each pilot has a different personality. A normal ability to face reality, handle anxiety, and think rationally under pressure varies over a range. How a particular pilot reacts to a threat may depend on training and experience and may vary considerably. When a threat appears and calls for a decision, two hazardous attitudes may come into play. A pilot might react impulsively without due consideration or with resignation and not respond in a timely manner. Either extreme may increase workload and confusion and may not address a threat or error properly.

What is an Undesired Aircraft State?

Flight crew error creates an undesired aircraft state described as:

- Incorrect aircraft position, speed, attitude, or configuration.
- An in-flight situation that causes pilot confusion and increased workload.
- Reduced safety margins and increased risk from threats or errors.

Defenses against Threats, Errors, and Undesired Aircraft States

When a pilot perceives a flight condition that requires attention, the pilot may know what to do immediately or may need time to process alternatives. The pilot may utilize several different strategies and defenses to manage risk while in the air.

Defenses Provided to the Pilot or Crew

A manufacturer, employer, or a flight school may provide defenses to pilots. Examples include checklists, operating limitations, minimum pilot qualifications, standard operating procedures, and insurance requirements. Regardless of the flight mission, some defenses will always be predetermined.

Checklists, Standard Operating Procedures, and Best Practices

Like the aircraft, its approved checklists are normally provided. The manufacturer's approved checklists, placards, and emergency procedures provide a basic defense against threats, errors, or undesired aircraft states. Many flight schools, flying clubs, and larger flight departments may develop checklists and standard operating procedures (SOPs) that enhance the procedures provided by the manufacturer. Many aircraft owners participate in type-specific owner organizations that develop and share best practices. A short video on developing a checklist that includes optional or aftermarket equipment is available here.

Utilizing a Second Pilot or Person

Even when flying a single-pilot aircraft, a pilot may choose to fly with a second pilot. The second pilot may be a flight instructor or another pilot who can perform some flight duties. The pilot can also assign specific duties to a passenger who can help monitor certain conditions or read a checklist. Pilots should consider how to use an additional person appropriately since a resource could also introduce threats.

External Resources

Flight service personnel are a valuable resource, especially for weather avoidance and flight plan changes. Air traffic control can assist pilots with traffic avoidance, weather avoidance, terrain avoidance, and navigation. However, ATC workload or equipment limitations affect the amount of assistance they can provide. In larger operations, a dispatch or company operations center can normally coordinate all communications and assistance.

Defenses Provided by the Pilot or Crew

Certain pilot behaviors defend against threats and errors.

Clear Communication and Briefings

Whether operating as a single pilot or as part of a crew, clear and concise communication is the foundation for sharing information and conveying intentions. When communicating with ATC or during crew briefings, each pilot should agree on the plan of action, ask for clarification, and question any inconsistency.

Effective Situational Awareness

Situational awareness may include knowing:

- Aircraft position
- Flight Path
- Status of other aircraft in the area
- Status of the environment
- Human factors in play

Planning for What Comes Next

Situational awareness allows the pilot to plan for what will happen next and to stay ahead of the aircraft. A forward-looking plan also provides for early detection of any deviation from expectations.

Time Management

On the ground, the pilot has the option to stop the aircraft. Pilots can always resume taxi after addressing an issue. Once airborne, budgeting time, prioritizing tasks, or slowing aircraft speed may allow sufficient time to complete tasks without error. A pilot feeling rushed while being vectored for an approach can request a delay or a vector that gives more time for completing checklists or configuring the aircraft.

Teamwork

Pilots may normally communicate with Flight Service and ATC. Some operators also have dispatchers available who track and assist flights. These external contacts are part of a team and a resource that can provide in-flight assistance. However, in a critical situation during any flight, declaring an emergency results in additional assistance and priority handling.

When the flight involves more than one pilot, crew resource management principles should be used. Typically, this allows one pilot focus on flight path management while the second pilot monitors the flight and accomplishes other tasks. However, the pilots should communicate their reasoning, intentions, and actions to allow for discussion, agreement, and verification.

Automation Management

Managing automation can reduce workload and improve situational awareness if understood and used properly. Automation management will be discussed in greater detail in Chapter 7, Automation & Flight Path Management.

Flying Skills (The Last Resort)

Employing this defense becomes necessary after experiencing an undesired aircraft state that cannot be remedied with other defenses alone. Ability to take full control of the aircraft and return to safe flying parameters is of critical importance.

Pilots should always train, remain current, remain proficient, improve knowledge, employ risk management, and be ready to handle any situation that could occur. Effective risk management and threat and error management usually prevent occurrences of an undesired aircraft state that may require a pilot to rely solely on flying skills as a defense.

Proficiency

A pilot who remains proficient is better prepared to defend against threats, errors, and undesired aircraft states. This can be depicted in the context of a Swiss cheese model. Each piece of Swiss cheese is a component of the defense against threats, errors, and undesired aircraft states. [*Figure 6-1*] Each of the holes in the cheese is a weakness in those defenses. A greater level of proficiency reduces the likelihood the holes will align.

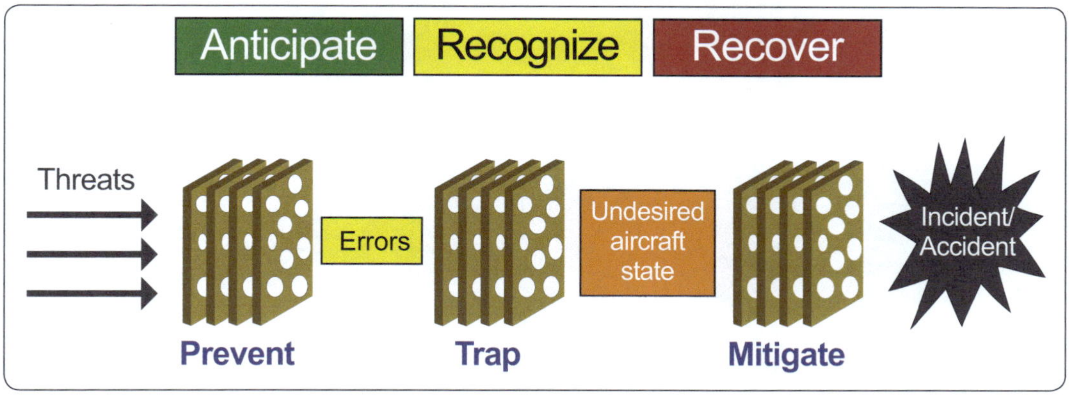

Figure 6-1. *The Swiss cheese model.*

Discipline

Discipline stems from good training and habit patterns. A disciplined pilot will perform a task in a similar manner each time regardless of proficiency. For example, completing the preflight inspection of the aircraft by using and following the approved checklist every time is a mark of discipline. Discipline also affects aeronautical decision-making. A disciplined pilot will be guarded and inoculated against hazardous attitudes and operational pitfalls, as shown in *Figure 6-2*. In general, a disciplined pilot will always do the right thing. Just like proficiency, discipline will lessen the likelihood that a threat or error will find a path through the pilot defenses.

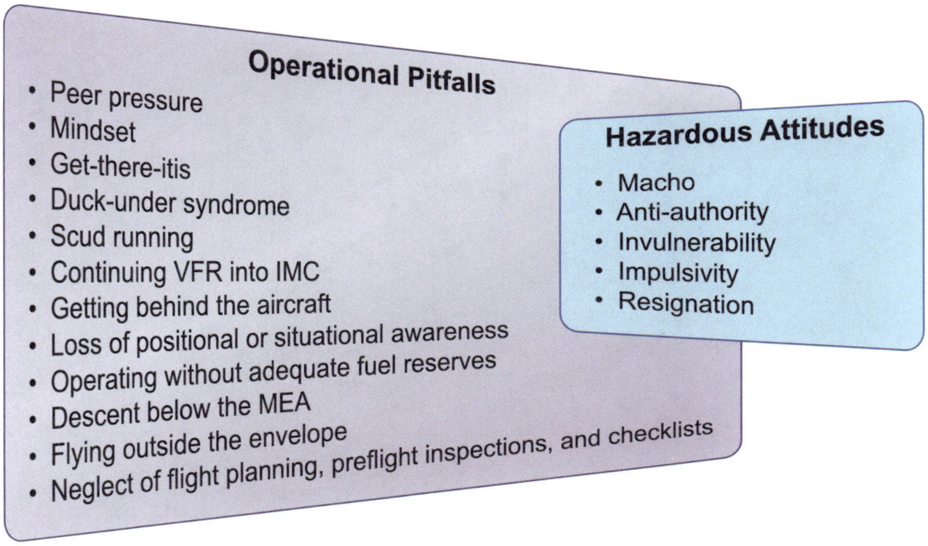

Figure 6-2. *Operational Pitfalls and Hazardous Attitudes.*

Chapter Summary

Defenses against threats and errors are either provided to the pilot or provided by the pilot. Pilots should perceive threats and errors and respond appropriately. The response may require the use of an appropriate checklist or may require more complex decision-making. A trained, proficient, and disciplined pilot uses appropriate threat and error management strategies to prevent or recover from an undesired aircraft state.

Chapter 7: Automation & Flight Path Management

Introduction

Automation systems provide an interface allowing the pilot to set a desired aircraft state. The system takes pilot input and aircraft information into account, develops a logical solution, and acts to fulfill the programmed objectives without continuous input from the pilot. When used properly, automation can reduce workload, enhance situational awareness, and allow the pilot to focus more attention on the aircraft flight path. Aircraft automation designs range from basic control of one system to complex integration of many systems.

At the start of the age of automation, engineers designed automation into individual systems. For example, a pilot might hold a switch and monitor an indicator to obtain a desired flap setting in an aircraft equipped with electric flaps. Automation of this system included a series of detents for the flap switch such that the pilot could select the desired flap setting. The system sensed the input and automatically positioned the flaps as set by the pilot. This system reduced the time and attention needed to set flaps.

With the advent of computers, networks, and conversion between analog and digital signals, it became possible to control many functions at the same time. These systems, available for some time in transport category aircraft, are now widely available in general aviation aircraft. This chapter discusses how the use of these systems can affect safety.

Some automation technologies include:

- Flight management systems that use a database to navigate and sequence through a series of waypoints, which interface with an autopilot. [*Figure 7-1*]
- Aircraft pressurization systems that operate without pilot adjustment during flight.
- Automated fuel management systems that operate without pilot intervention during normal operations.
- Auto-throttles and digital engine controls.
- Avionics systems that load flight plan information from a database or from an outside source.

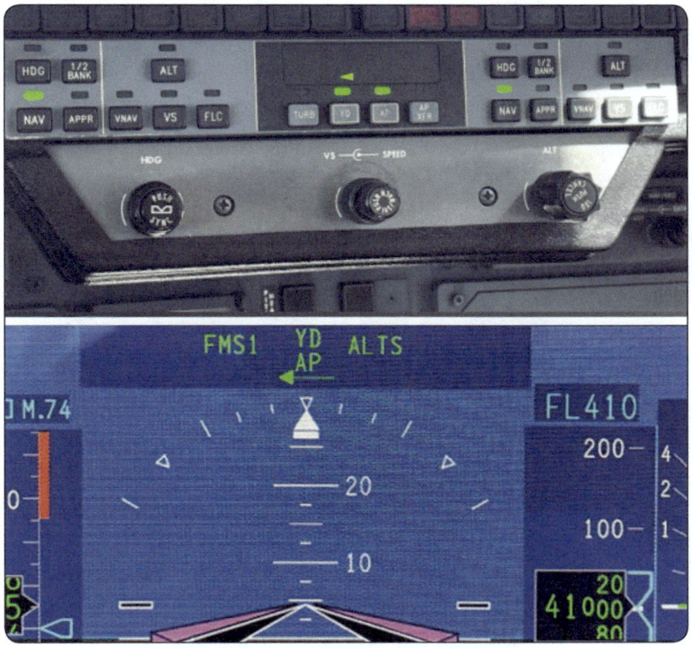

Figure 7-1. *Autopilot interface.*

Reliance on Automation

The use of automation comes with certain cautions. Automation should reduce workload, but in some instances, it may create more work, confusion, and contribute to errors. At other times, automation may lull pilots into complacency. Pilots who consistently rely on an autopilot for flight path management may experience degraded ability to fly manually when required to do so. For example, when flying in icing conditions, an automated system may make control inputs to compensate for ice accumulation. However, if the system exceeds its limits, it could disconnect and leave the aircraft in an undesired state. A pilot who has become unaccustomed to manual flight may not be prepared to handle the situation.

Reprogramming tasks that occur unexpectedly can trigger pilot errors, which may result in flight path deviations or other undesired aircraft states. Pilots should anticipate the need to fly manually and be prepared to maintain the desired flight path when manual control becomes necessary.

Pilots who use automation should train and practice for various scenarios in order to avoid becoming overly distracted when making a programming change or correcting an error. Being startled or confused by a programming mistake or automation malfunction occurs less often when the pilot has the capability for transition to manual flight. If the automation is not functioning according to expectation, the pilot may reduce the level of automation, fly manually, and take time to resolve the condition.

Balancing Automated & Manual Flight

Pilots choose the level of flight path automation. Risk management strategies suggest using automation as an aid to manage workload rather than to compensate for lack of proficiency. A balance of automated and manual flight that takes workload and proficiency into consideration gives the pilot greater opportunity to monitor the flight path and aircraft state.

Choosing the appropriate level of automation for the task and adjusting as circumstances dictate is essential to effective use of automation. One of the most common errors is failing to move to lower levels of automation suitable to a changing environment.

For example, a pilot may track an approach course adequately using manual control inputs. However, the pilot may also need to listen to and record the Automatic Terminal Information Service (ATIS), retrieve and load an instrument approach procedure, prepare for the instrument approach, and accomplish the appropriate checklists. These tasks will increase workload and divert pilot attention from monitoring and controlling the flight path. If using an autopilot to track the approach, the automation performs the control inputs and allows the pilot to complete other tasks quickly and efficiently.

Continuing the scenario above, the pilot loads the instrument approach and decides to remain on autopilot. However, after the aircraft passes the initial approach fix, ATC cancels the approach clearance. ATC provides vectors and tells the pilot to expect to hold. In this situation, the pilot may select basic autopilot modes that control heading and altitude in order to comply with the assignment from ATC. The lower level of automation allows the pilot to program and configure the aircraft for an unexpected change while keeping the flightpath and aircraft state under control.

Pilots may sometimes choose to disengage the automation and fly the aircraft manually to maintain proficiency.

Interacting with Automation

Regardless of the level of automation, pilots should consider the following series of steps: [*Figure 7-2*]

1. Anticipate – Understand the system well enough to know what should happen before pushing a button or turning a knob.

2. Act – Execute button pushes and knob turns to implement the desired automation.

3. Verify – Ensure the aircraft or avionics performs as expected.

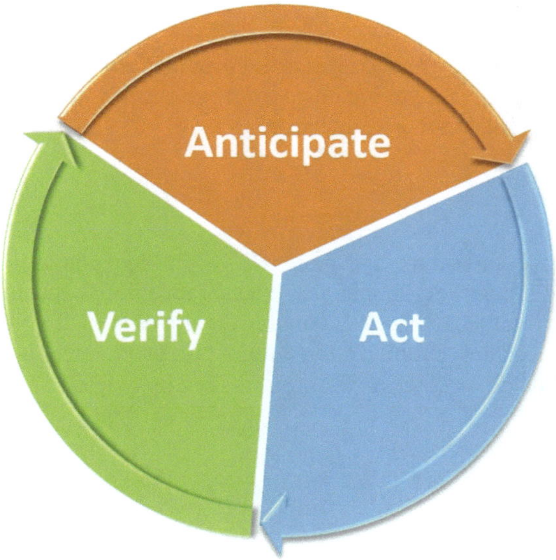

Figure 7-2. *Steps for interacting with automation*

Understanding autopilot function and logic allows the pilot to anticipate, act, and verify the autopilot performs as expected. *Figure 7-3* shows a typical flight mode annunciator displayed on the primary flight display (PFD) of a general aviation integrated flight deck. A pilot without adequate training may not anticipate that a change or disruption of the navigation source may reduce the level of automation, and horizontal flight path control may default to wings level mode. If this should occur unexpectedly, it could lead to increased workload, confusion, or result in an undesired aircraft state.

Figure 7-3. *Flight mode annunciators in green indicate the autopilot is engaged in heading "HDG" and altitude "ALT" mode, maintaining 9,000 feet MSL. The white "LOC" and "GS" annunciators indicate approach mode is armed but not engaged.*

Failure to Anticipate, Act, & Verify

Automation offers increased safety with enhanced situational awareness. However, these systems make it possible for a pilot to become complacent, unprepared, or lose situational awareness. If this occurs and an unexpected change in flight plan is needed, workload and confusion may suddenly increase.

In a 1995 fatal accident in Colombia, a flight crew was unexpectedly cleared for an approach, lost situational awareness, and crashed into mountainous terrain. The accident summary cites failure of the flight crew to revert to basic radio navigation at the time when the FMS-assisted navigation became confusing and created an excessive workload in a critical phase of the flight. The system flew on a programmed path into a mountain, resulting in many fatalities. A narrative of the accident is available here.

As part of a lack of situational awareness, the workload and confusion resulted in the crew failing to retract the aircraft speed brakes when they became aware of the terrain ahead and after adding full thrust. This prevented the aircraft from climbing above the slope of the mountain ahead.

Integrated Flight Path Automation Systems

Use of automation is an excellent risk control measure when flying in a variety of flight environments where the pilot has a high workload. For example, autopilots are often very useful during complex single-pilot operations. While the use of automation helps reduce risks associated with other hazards, a lack of proficiency with automation may become its own hazard and introduce unique risks. While pilots often rely on the autopilot, they also need to be able to fly the aircraft manually within appropriate standards.

Pilots should train and practice using automation under VFR with an appropriately qualified and knowledgeable flight instructor before attempting IFR flight. In addition, using a flight simulation training device provides the opportunity to practice and repeat automation procedures with a simulated high workload. Through appropriate training and practice, pilots learn to operate autopilot systems with ease and in a routine manner.

Knowledge of system limitations and operating restrictions is also important. Pilots should know emergency procedures pertaining to disconnecting the autopilot as well as being able to locate appropriate checklists. Reviewing the system documentation and aircraft flight manual supplements helps develop this knowledge.

Chapter Summary

The increased use of automated systems, autopilots, and integrated flight decks help pilots manage an aircraft's flight path. While an autopilot is engaged, a pilot's attention should not disengage. Pilots need to maintain situational awareness and appropriate focus on the progress of the flight at all times. Balancing the use of automation with manual flying skills is necessary in case a particular situation requires pilot intervention. Using automation proficiently and at the appropriate level reduces risk and helps prevent incidents and accidents.

Chapter 8: Aeronautical Decision-Making in Flight

Introduction

This chapter focuses on the pilot aeronautical decision-making (ADM) skills used to mitigate risk factors while in flight. Advisory Circular (AC) 60-22, Aeronautical Decision-Making [*Figure 8-1*], provides additional information, background references, definitions, and other pertinent information about ADM training in the general aviation environment and is available here.

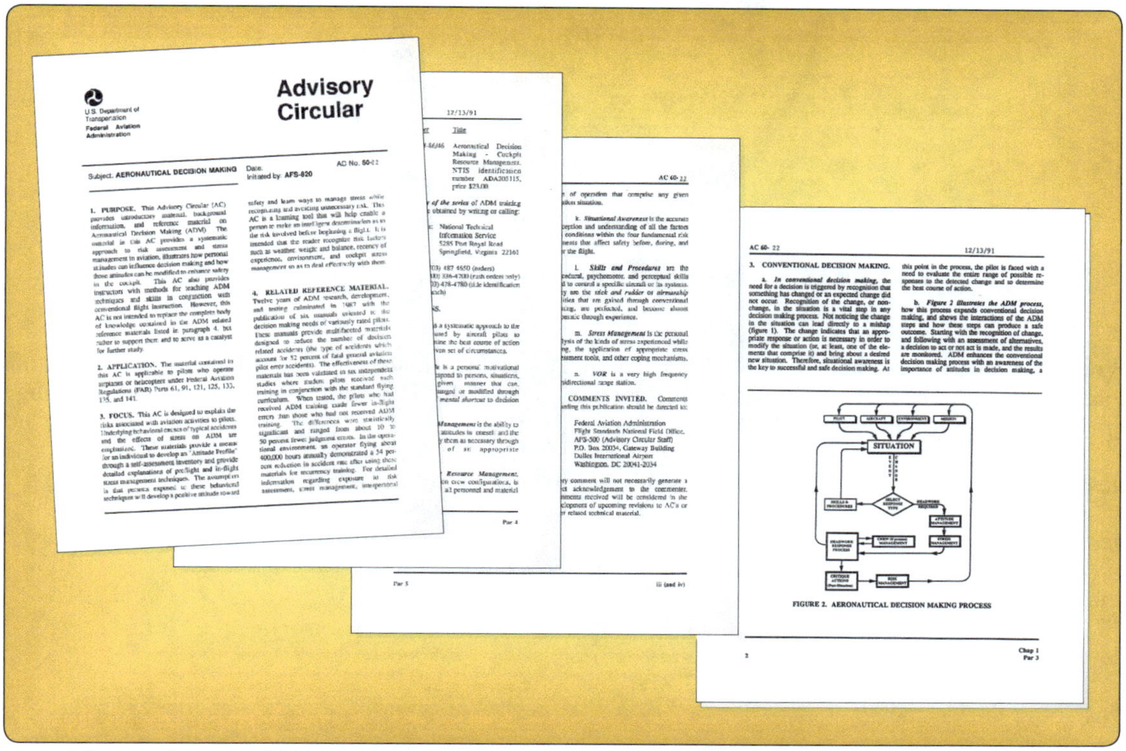

Figure 8-1. *Advisory Circular (AC) 60-22, Aeronautical Decision-Making, includes a wealth of information for pilots.*

Accidents still occur despite advances in training methods, aircraft technology, and services available to pilots. Despite improvements in training and technology, human error remains an issue. ADM provides a foundation, which should help pilots avoid making errors in judgment.

Aeronautical decision-making (ADM) provides pilots with a structured framework of processes and procedures, which have a positive effect on managing hazards. ADM does not eliminate hazards, but helps the pilot address hazards and associated risks that threaten the safety of flight. ADM describes the ongoing process used by pilots to determine the best course of action when facing a given set of circumstances.

ADM Background

Before the development of ADM training, consensus held that good judgment resulted from experience gained during hours of accident-free flying. However, research done during the 1980s indicated that including ADM in training significantly reduced judgment errors among student pilots. In addition, an operator flying about 400,000 hours annually demonstrated a 54 percent reduction in the accident rate after adding ADM to recurrent training. Since ADM enhances safety, the Federal Aviation Administration (FAA) requires ADM training and testing.

Analytical Decision-Making

Several closed-loop models describe steps pilots should take when making decisions. For example, AC 60-22 contains information on the DECIDE Model, which pilots may wish to study and consider using. The following discussion describes the simpler 3P model, which stands for Perceive, Process, and Perform. [*Figure 8-2*] Using this model in flight continues the risk management activity taken before flight, and allows the pilot to address additional hazards while dealing with a higher workload.

Figure 8-2. *The illustration shows how the 3P model is used in decision-making.*

Perceive: While en route, for example, a pilot checks data-link weather on an electronic flight bag and sees thunderstorms developing ahead. The pilot perceives this as a significant hazard since the likelihood of a thunderstorm affecting the aircraft could be high and the consequences could be severe.

Process: The pilot considers the options available to mitigate the threat. Choices may include:

- Diverting to a nearby airport
- Turning back, if conditions allow
- Rerouting the flight to avoid the thunderstorms
- Flying above the weather.

During analytical decision-making, the pilot evaluates the pros and cons associated with each option and chooses one that should adequately reduce the level of risk. For example, the aircraft may not have the equipment or capability to fly above the weather or there might not be enough fuel on board for a significant reroute. In that case, the pilot excludes those two options. What the pilot decides depends on the available choices, training, experience, conditions, equipment, and pilot ability.

Analytical decision-making leads to an option likely to result in a safe outcome. Pilots should consider the following items less important than safety:

1. Being on time
2. Inconveniencing passengers
3. Inconveniencing persons waiting at the destination
4. Continuing to the original destination

Perform: After choosing a viable option, the pilot executes the changes. The choice made should lead to a safe outcome.

Effective risk management models utilize a closed-loop process. The closed-loop nature of the 3P model requires a periodic check to verify successful mitigation of the risk. If the pilot perceives insufficient mitigation of that risk or detects a new hazard, the process and analysis resumes.

Naturalistic Decision-Making

Experienced pilots use naturalistic decision-making when the time available precludes a more formal analytical process. In this type of scenario, pilots first assess whether the given situation strikes them as familiar. Rather than analyze the pros and cons of different actions, a pilot might start with a course of action that seems workable based on previously encountered patterns.

In this type of decision-making, pilots may recall previous events and choose a course of action based on expectations. In the following scenario, a pilot's familiarity with a previous incident led to a successful naturalistic decision.

A turkey vulture impacted the front fan of a jet engine shortly after takeoff and destroyed the engine. Several titanium fan blades departed the aircraft and the cabin filled with smoke. The crew landed safely after donning masks and goggles. The impact was forceful enough to leave an impression of the feathers on some of the remaining blades. [*Figure 8-3*]

Figure 8-3. *Sheared off titanium fan blade with feather impressions.*

Years later, a pilot who investigated this bird strike was flying a turbojet. When a large bird appeared in the departure path, the pilot delayed rotation a few seconds, and the airplane flew under the bird without incident. Visualizing what could happen, knowing that there were no obstacles ahead, sensing that a short delay would not exceed any limitations, and remembering that instructors mentioned that pilots might delay rotation if conditions warrant, the pilot made a split-second decision to extend the takeoff roll beyond rotation speed.

In summary, naturalistic decision-making improves with training and experience, and it is not a replacement for memory items or a checklist procedure. Pilots typically use naturalistic decision-making when a situation requires immediate action and is not covered by an existing procedure.

Single-Pilot Resource Management

Single-pilot resource management (SRM) specifically refers to appropriate management of all resources available to the single pilot. SRM includes competencies such as situational awareness, communication skills, teamwork, task allocation, aeronautical decision-making, risk management, controlled flight into terrain (CFIT) awareness, and automation management. Resources are found both inside and outside the aircraft. Many of the concepts are similar to crew resource management (CRM).

Learning to recognize these resources is an essential part of SRM. In addition, a pilot should evaluate whether there is time to use a particular resource. For example, ATC assistance may be very useful if a pilot becomes lost, but there may be no time to contact ATC in an emergency. During an emergency, a pilot needs to prioritize tasks and manage workload.

Many older aircraft may have modern equipment installed, which require a flight manual supplement. This equipment can be a valuable single-pilot resource if the pilot uses the equipment proficiently and adjusts procedures appropriately. In some cases, the procedures for new equipment affect the aircraft checklists. A short video on modern installations and checklist management is available here.

In a single-pilot operation, pilots often gather, organize, and manage available resources before flight to make it easier to assess and manage risks and make informed aeronautical decisions. The comprehensive planning and preparation activities described earlier in chapters 3, 4, and 5 facilitate SRM. If the pilot prepares for scenarios that may occur during a flight, such as a diversion or precautionary landing, it becomes easier to consider and perform that option with the needed information at hand. For example, while en route to an airport the aircraft alternator fails. After completing the appropriate checklist, the alternator remains off line, and the battery will only provide electricity for a short time. The pilot decides to divert to the nearest suitable airport. Does the pilot know the destinations along the route of flight that qualify? Did the pilot organize personal and flight deck resources to access information such as communication frequencies and navigation aids for the available airports? By considering and organizing information before flight, the single pilot may perform such tasks with crew-like efficiency.

Chapter Summary

Aeronautical decision-making occurs during all aspects of flight and begins during flight planning. When in flight, however, pilots learn to deal with any threat using appropriate analytical thinking. The analytical process prevails unless time pressure and lack of an existing procedure calls for naturalistic decision-making. The 3P model illustrates a closed-loop process that pilots use to reinforce appropriate decision-making. Several models address ADM, and pilots should study and use the model they find effective.

Appendix Introduction

Scope

Appendices A through D are designed to supplement the material in this handbook. To take full advantage of the appendices, readers should become familiar with the material in Chapters 2, 3, 4, and 5.

The information in these appendices is designed to cover single-pilot operation of general aviation aircraft. While multi-crew operations may utilize concepts and programs such as crew resource management (CRM), safety management systems (SMS), and advanced qualification programs (AQP), these programs also use risk mitigation principles discussed in this handbook.

How to Use

Each appendix accomplishes a specific purpose.

Appendix A, Risk Management Training, suggests integration of risk management into initial, recurrent, and specialized flight training. Pilots should work with flight instructors to ensure risk management is included in initial training, training for additional ratings, and currency events as appropriate. For example, a pilot in need of a flight review or instrument proficiency check (IPC) may request a risk-based review or check. Instructors should refer to Chapter 10 of the Aviation Instructor's Handbook (FAA-H-8083-9, latest edition) to review teaching risk management.

Appendix B, Risk Management Tools, lists assessment tools discussed in Chapters 3, 4, and 5. These include both numerical and non-numerical flight risk assessment tools, models, checklists, and risk assessment matrix discussed in the chapters. This section can be used as a reference while reviewing the cases and examples in Appendices C and D.

Appendix C, Risk Management Accident Case Studies, reviews several fatal accidents from a risk management perspective. Appendix C includes an analysis of four accidents, which include recreational flying, single-pilot operation of turbine-powered airplanes, and a helicopter operation.

Appendix D, Risk Management Exercises, contains four hypothetical scenarios. Questions are posed asking the reader to conduct a risk analysis for each scenario. A solution is not provided as was done in Appendix C, and the reader may develop a risk analysis for each scenario as an exercise.

Using Appendices as a Workbook

The appendices provide an opportunity to apply the concepts covered in this handbook. These appendices bridge the knowledge in this handbook, further risk management training, and the type of preparation that should occur before flight. For maximum benefit, pilots should consider taking a risk management course.

Appendix A: Risk Management Training

Integrating Risk Management Training and Other Training Requirements

Application of risk management principles becomes more effective after specific training for this purpose. Sources of risk management training include flight or ground instructors, schools, and commercial sources.

The effectiveness of risk management training increases when integrated with the knowledge, risk, and skill requirements contained in the applicable Airman Certification Standards (ACS).

Risk management training will also be more effective if it is integrated with other SRM skills such as automation management, task and workload management, and situational awareness. These higher order thinking skills are crucial to operating safely in today's aviation environment.

Flight reviews, instrument proficiency checks, and other evaluation activities include the certification requirements for risk management. These events should use scenarios designed to address the hazards and associated risks relevant to the pilot. For example, external pressures could be simulated using a "what if" scenario that might arise for a pilot who regularly flies associates or family to events that cannot be rescheduled.

Appendix B: Risk Management Tools

Risk Assessment Tools Identifying, Assessing, & Mitigating Risk

This appendix contains tools readers may use to review the accident and case study examples in Appendices C and D from an academic risk management perspective. For example, *Figure B-1* depicts the PAVE checklist. Many of the tools described in this appendix work to the same end, and pilots may use a combination of tools to manage risk. Instructors normally provide training and guidance on the appropriate use of these tools.

Pilot

- A pilot must continually make decisions about competency, condition of health, mental and emotional state, level of fatigue, and many other variables. For example, a pilot may be called early in the morning to make a long flight. If a pilot has had only a few hours of sleep and is concerned that the sinus congestion being experienced could be the onset of a cold, it would be prudent to consider if the flight could be accomplished safely.
- A pilot had only 4 hours of sleep the night before being asked by the boss to fly to a meeting in a city 750 miles away. The reported weather was marginal and not expected to improve. After assessing fitness as a pilot, it was decided that it would not be wise to make the flight. The boss was initially unhappy, but was later convinced by the pilot that the risks involved were unacceptable.

Aircraft

- A pilot frequently bases decisions on evaluation of the airplane, such as performance, equipment, or airworthiness.
- During a preflight, a pilot noticed a small amount of oil dripping from the bottom of the cowling. Although the quantity of oil seemed insignificant at the time, the pilot decided to delay the takeoff and have a mechanic check the source of the oil. The pilot's good judgment was confirmed when the mechanic found that one of the oil cooler hose fittings was loose.

EnVironment

- The environment encompasses many elements that are not pilot or airplane related, including such factors as weather, air traffic control (ATC), navigational aids (NAVAIDS), terrain, takeoff and landing areas, and surrounding obstacles. Weather is one element that can change drastically over time and distance.
- A pilot was landing a small airplane just after a heavy jet had departed a parallel runway. The pilot assumed that wake turbulence would not be a problem since landings had been performed under similar circumstances. Due to a combination of prevailing winds and wake turbulence from the heavy jet drifting across the landing runway, the airplane made a hard landing. The pilot made an error when assessing the flight environment.

External Pressures

- The interaction between the pilot, airplane, and the environment is greatly influenced by the purpose of each flight operation. The pilot must evaluate the three previous areas to decide on the desirability of undertaking or continuing the flight as planned. It is worth asking why the flight is being made, how critical it is to maintain the schedule, and if the trip is worth the risks.
- On a ferry flight to deliver an airplane from the factory, the pilot calculated the groundspeed and determined he would arrive at the destination with only 10 minutes of fuel remaining. A check of the weather revealed he would be flying into marginal weather conditions. By asking himself whether it was more critical to maintain the schedule or to arrive with an intact aircraft, the pilot decided to schedule a refuel stop even though it would mean he would not be able to keep to the schedule. He chose not to "stretch" the fuel supply in marginal weather conditions which could have resulted in an emergency landing.

Figure B-1. *The PAVE checklist.*

Risk Identification Tools

Pilots may also use the FRAT [*Figure B-2*], which incorporates the PAVE checklist to aid with hazard identification.

Flight Risk Assessment Tool

PAVE Area	Hazard	Risk	Likelihood	Severity	Composite Risk	Mitigation Results
Pilot "P"						
Capability						
Aeromedical						
Aircraft "A"						
Fuel/Range/Payload						
Equipment						
Performance						
Environment "V"						
Weather						
Terrain						
Airspace, ATC, Airports						
Night/Over Water						
External Pressure "E"						
Personal						
Business						

Figure B-2. *Non-numerical FRAT, which incorporates the PAVE checklist.*

The risk assessment matrix shown in *Figure B-3* provides a means to determine risk level. The risk likelihood and severity determine the overall level of risk for each hazard, after which various means to reduce unacceptable risk can be analyzed.

Risk Assessment Matrix

Likelihood	Severity: Catastrophic	Critical	Marginal	Negligible
Probable	High	High	Serious	
Occasional	High	Serious		
Remote	Serious	Medium		Low
Improbable				

Figure B-3. *Risk Assessment Matrix.*

The 3P model illustrated in *Figure B-4* allows for streamlined hazard identification and mitigation during in-flight operations. However, the "perceive" portion of the 3P model and PAVE checklist share a common purpose. Both serve to identify hazards.

Figure B-4. *3P process.*

Figure B-5. *3P "Perceive" analysis and PAVE checklist risk identification.*

Additional Risk Assessment Tools

The CARE checklist provides a breakdown of rationale pilots use during the 3P "process" stage [*Figure B-6*]. It includes a perspective of what could happen (consequences), what may be done to prevent an unwanted outcome (alternatives), a check of the actual conditions (reality), and an analysis of pilot motivation (external pressures).

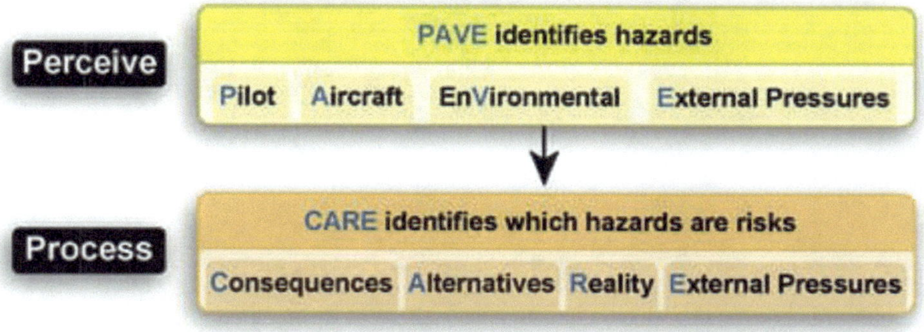

Figure B-6. *Process using the CARE checklist for risk assessment.*

Risk Mitigation Tools

The TEAM checklist shares the "perform" step in the 3P model as well as the "alternatives" component from the CARE checklist.

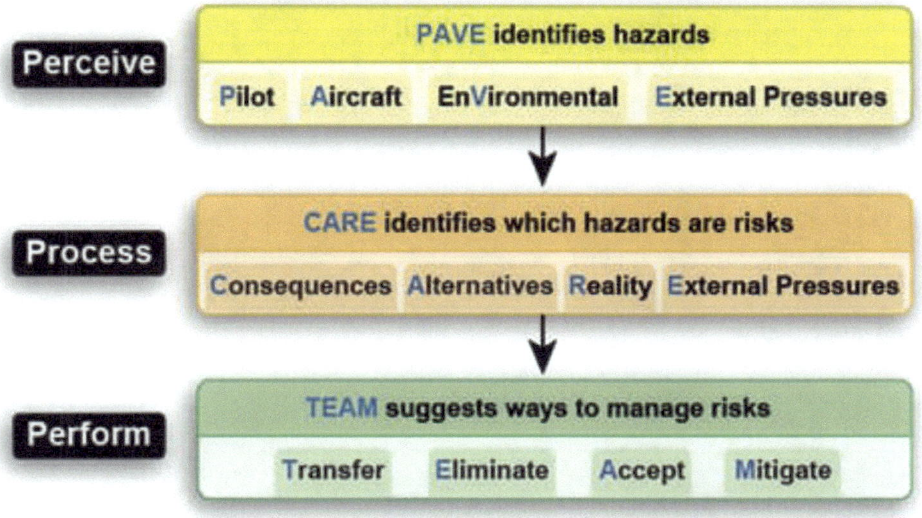

Figure B-7. *"Perform" using the TEAM checklist for risk mitigation.*

Analysis of hazards and associated risks may follow the six-step DECIDE Model shown in *Figure B-8*.

The DECIDE Model
1. **Detect.** The decision maker detects the fact that change has occurred.
2. **Estimate.** The decision maker estimates the need to counter or react to the change.
3. **Choose.** The decision maker chooses a desirable outcome (in terms of success) for the flight.
4 **Identify.** The decision maker identifies actions which could successfully control the change.
5. **Do.** The decision maker takes the necessary action.
6. **Evaluate.** The decision maker evaluates the effect(s) of his/her action countering the change.

Figure B-8. *The DECIDE Model.*

Appendix C: Accident Case Studies

General Information

The fatal accident profiles described below represent a range of general aviation activities. For additional accident information search the NTSB Aviation Accident Database here.

For each accident, a summary using the PAVE checklist highlights potential risk factors that, in retrospect, may teach something about decision-making. The analysis includes an assessment of risks, as well as potential mitigations that could have altered the outcome. Individuals may use a variety of other tools, models, and checklists including those outlined in Appendix B to perform a similar analysis.

The accident case studies outlined below involve single-pilot operations. Analysis of accidents involving flight crew operations could also include a discussion of crew interaction and resource management (CRM) principles.

Accident Profile 1: Fatal Accident in a Single-Engine Airplane with a Piston Engine

The following details pertain to this accident:

- Location: Veneta, OR (Crow-Mag airport, 33OR)
- Date: 06/23/2012
- NTSB Defining Event: Loss of lift
- NTSB Case File Number: WPR12FA274

NTSB Probable Cause

The pilot's failure to maintain adequate airspeed and altitude to clear trees during the initial climb after takeoff.

NTSB Factual Summary Excerpts (edited)

The pilot was carrying three passengers on a local scenic flight, and the aircraft was near maximum gross weight. Visual meteorological conditions prevailed at departure. The 3,100-foot turf runway had 3-inch or higher wet grass and there were 100-foot trees at the end of the runway. The pilot operating handbook (POH) showed approximately 1,700 feet required for a takeoff from a hard-surface runway over a 50-foot obstacle. The POH did not provide takeoff data for a turf runway with wet grass or a 100-foot obstacle.

After departure, the aircraft descended into the trees. A cell phone video taken from inside the aircraft recorded the sound of the stall warning just before the collision. Witnesses reported seeing the aircraft descend into the trees. All four occupants died during the crash. An autopsy toxicology report indicated the presence of marijuana in the pilot's bloodstream; however, the degree of pilot impairment could not be determined. The investigators could not find any aircraft defects that would have prevented it from achieving full power on takeoff.

Risk Identification, Assessment, and Mitigation

The hazards associated with this accident may involve all four categories of the PAVE checklist. However, environmental and aircraft performance hazards may have generated the highest risk levels.

The primary environment hazards in this accident are the 100-foot trees at the end of the runway and the wet-grass turf runway. These environmental factors, coupled with an aircraft hazard arising from takeoff and climb performance limitations, generated the risk that may explain the accident. An external pressure hazard associated with pleasing the passengers may have existed.

A pilot aeromedical hazard existed due to marijuana use. There is evidence taking illicit drugs significantly elevates the risk of having an aviation accident. Even though the Drug Enforcement Administration (DEA) defines marijuana as a Schedule I drug on its controlled substances list, states have taken steps to allow the possession, sale, and use of marijuana within their borders. The FAA has stated, "Marijuana is an illicit drug per federal law, and its use by airmen is prohibited."

The risk severity generated by the collision potential with the trees is "catastrophic" because it resulted in loss of life. Given the environment and aircraft performance limitations that the pilot could have reasonably anticipated, the likelihood of the risk was at least "occasional," that is, it would probably occur sometime. Consulting the risk assessment matrix, the resulting risk is high (red) and requires mitigation to a lower level of likelihood and/or severity.

Because the airplane was located at the turf airport, avoiding risk generated by the trees warranted careful consideration. The pilot could have greatly reduced the likelihood of an accident by flying the aircraft solo to the nearby Eugene, OR (EUG) airport to pick up the passengers [*Figure C-1*]. This single action addresses both the environmental and aircraft performance risks. This could also have reduced the external pressures.

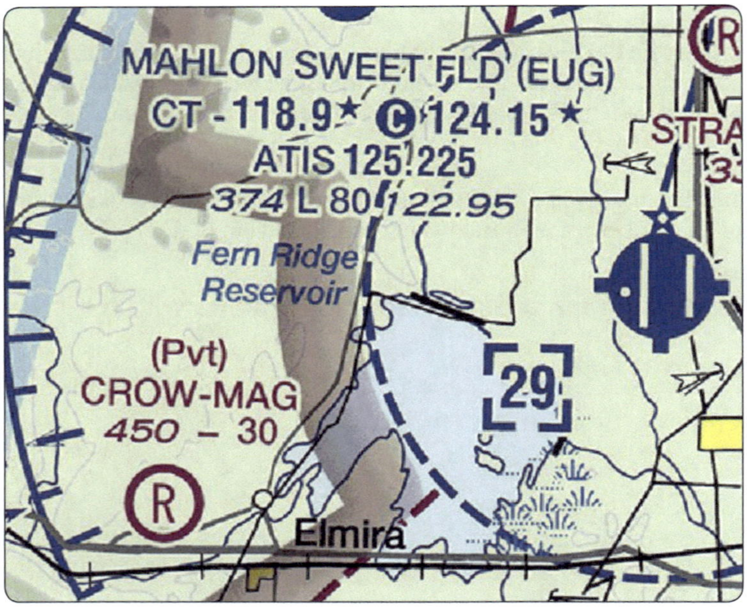

Figure C-1. *Sectional chart excerpt.*

Accident Profile 2: Fatal Accident, Turboprop-Powered, Transportation

The following details pertain to this accident:

- Location: Morristown, NJ
- Date: 12/20/2011
- NTSB Defining Event: Loss of control in-flight
- NTSB Case File Number: ERA12FA115

NTSB Probable Cause

The airplane's encounter with severe icing conditions that were characterized by high ice accretion rates and the pilot's failure to use command authority to depart the icing conditions in an expeditious manner, which resulted in a loss of airplane control.

NTSB Factual Summary Excerpts (edited)

The pilot departed Teterboro, NJ (TEB) on an IFR flight plan to Atlanta, GA (PDK). No evidence of a weather briefing was found, although the pilot may have obtained weather information from non-government sources. There was an AIRMET for moderate icing in northern New Jersey and westward from the freezing level (2,000 to 8,000 feet) to 20,000 feet. There were numerous pilot reports of moderate to severe icing and a Center Weather Advisory (CWA) issued, as depicted in *Figure C-2*.

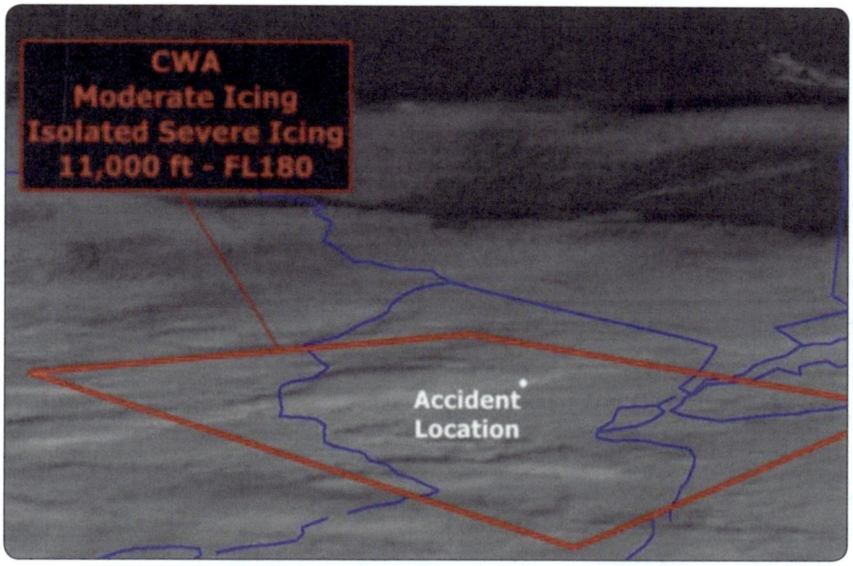

Figure C-2. *CWA moderate to severe icing area.*

The pilot reported entering light icing at 16,800 feet and requested a higher altitude. There was a delay before air traffic control subsequently approved a climb to Flight Level 200. The radar track showed the airplane reached a peak altitude of 17,800 feet before beginning a rapid descent. The aircraft disintegrated during the descent and all five occupants perished. The airplane's flight manual included a warning that the aircraft was not approved for flight in severe icing conditions.

Risk Identification, Assessment, and Mitigation

No pilot risk factors were identified. The pilot was qualified in the aircraft and had recently attended recurrent training. As with any transportation flight, there may have been external pressures to complete the flight as planned.

The severity of the combined risk is catastrophic because it resulted in the loss of five lives. Given the severity of the icing, the length of exposure, and the warning in the airplane's flight manual, the likelihood of the event was at least "occasional," meaning it would probably occur sometime. Thus, the overall risk level was high and needed mitigation.

How could the pilot have mitigated the risk factors on this flight? One way may have been to file for 10,000 feet to stay under the icing conditions. The pilot could maintain this altitude until exiting the severe icing area somewhere in southern New Jersey. This would have decreased fuel efficiency, but it would not have taken much time to reach an area without icing. At that time, the pilot could request a climb to a more fuel-efficient altitude. While the lower altitude may generate a requirement for a fuel stop, that stop represents an inconvenience only.

Accident Profile 3: Fatal Accident, Helicopter, Personal Flight

The following details pertain to this accident:

- Location: Panacea, FL
- Date: 02/08/2014
- NTSB Defining Event: Collision during takeoff/land
- NTSB Case File Number: ERA14FA115

NTSB Probable Cause

The pilot's failure to maintain adequate clearance from trees during a takeoff at night. Contributing to the accident was the pilot's lack of recent night flight experience.

NTSB Factual Summary Excerpts (edited)

The pilot and two passengers flew from the Tallahassee, FL airport (TLH) to the nearby Wakulla County Airport (2J0). The purpose of the flight was to dine at the restaurant across the street. It was dusk when they arrived at 2J0.

After dinner, they returned to the helicopter for the return flight. The Wakulla airport and the area around it were poorly lit, and after liftoff, the helicopter impacted 50-foot trees about 350 feet from the liftoff point. The pilot and one passenger suffered fatal injuries and the other passenger was severely injured.

The pilot had only one hour of night flight experience in the previous 11 months and did not possess an instrument rating. Witnesses to the accident stated the area around the airport was dark or "very dark." The pilot was taking a disqualifying drug that can cause drowsiness, although the NTSB did not assert this as a factor in the accident.

The surviving passenger stated that the pilot was in a hurry to return home and spend time with his daughter.

Risk Identification, Assessment, and Mitigation

At least three of the four risk categories in the PAVE checklist may relate to this accident. The pilot had minimal night currency for this flight. In addition, aeromedical factors may have affected the pilot's perception of the environment.

The airport environment hazard contributed to the risk present at takeoff. The 50-foot trees near the takeoff zone resulted in a normal takeoff and climb that did not provide safe clearance during climb out. A hovering takeoff and climb also might have been hazardous at night in a dark environment.

External pressures relate to the pilot's desire to return as soon as possible. Perhaps this caused him to rush through the start-up and liftoff with reduced situational awareness of the airport environment.

The collective risk severity level for this accident was catastrophic. The risk likelihood was at least occasional, producing a high overall risk level. Avoiding nighttime operations at this particular airport could have been a key mitigation.

Accident Profile 4: Fatal Turbojet-Powered Airplane Accident

The following details pertain to this accident:

- Location: Cleveland, OH
- Date: 12/29/2016
- NTSB Defining Event: Loss of control in-flight
- NTSB Case File Number: CEN17FA072

NTSB Probable Cause

Controlled flight into terrain due to pilot spatial disorientation. Contributing to the accident was pilot fatigue, mode confusion related to the status of the autopilot, and negative learning transfer due to flight guidance panel and attitude indicator differences from the pilot's previous experience.

NTSB Factual Summary Excerpts (edited)

The pilot and five passengers flew to the Burke Lakefront Airport (BKL) earlier to attend a sporting event. They arrived back at BKL around 2230 for the return flight to Columbus, Ohio. Although BKL was VFR, the ceiling was 2300 feet and the departure took place in full darkness. Within two minutes after takeoff, the single pilot lost control of the aircraft. The radar track showed the aircraft climbing through its assigned altitude and then flying erratically before plunging into Lake Erie with a descent rate of about 6,000 feet per minute.

The pilot had been awake for 17 hours at takeoff. He had recently transitioned from another small jet and completed aircraft and simulator training, resulting in a single-pilot type rating only three weeks before the accident. According to his instructors, he had been taught to operate using the autopilot most of the time. He may have suffered from mode confusion regarding the configuration and status of the autopilot in the new aircraft, and may not have verified autopilot engagement. He may also have experienced external pressure to return to Columbus that evening.

Risk Identification, Assessment, and Mitigation

Several categories on the PAVE checklist may apply to this accident. The pilot may have been fatigued. It is likely that his expectation and that of the passengers was to return to Columbus immediately after the event. After departure, he may have unconsciously applied procedures appropriate to his previous experience. The nighttime environment and departure over the lake required the pilot to both monitor the flight instruments and deal with the automation.

The catastrophic consequences associated with this accident, when combined with at least occasional likelihood, created a high-risk level for loss of control. In hindsight, having a second pilot or "mentor pilot" for this flight may have reduced the likelihood of loss of control. In addition, remaining overnight in Cleveland would have provided needed rest for the pilot and allowed for a departure during daylight, which also could have reduced the likelihood of loss of control.

Appendix D: Risk Management Exercises

Four Scenarios

This appendix includes four hypothetical scenarios to illustrate the cycle of risk management including risk identification, assessment, and mitigation. While similar to the accident scenarios in Appendix C, the following case studies do not include a risk analysis. Instead, the reader may conduct a risk analysis and consider some "what-ifs." In this situation, there are no right or wrong answers and numerous solutions exist to mitigate risks to lower levels of likelihood and severity.

For each case study, the reader may consider the following items:

1. What are the potential hazards in the scenario?
2. What is the risk associated with each hazard?
3. What is the likelihood (probability) of each risk?
4. What is the severity (consequences) of each risk?
5. What is the overall risk level of each risk (red, yellow, green, white)?
6. What mitigations reduce the likelihood and severity?
7. What is the remaining level of risk after mitigation?
8. How does a pilot decide if sufficient risk mitigation has occurred or if further mitigation is needed?

Scenario 1: Recreational Aviation

A pilot is planning an annual flight to EAA Airventure in Oshkosh, WI (OSH) using a single-engine piston airplane. [*Figure D-1*]. It is a direct, non-stop (390 NM) from Chan Gurney Municipal (YKN) in Yankton, SD. Passengers include two friends who have never flown in a small aircraft. The planning began several days before the scheduled departure.

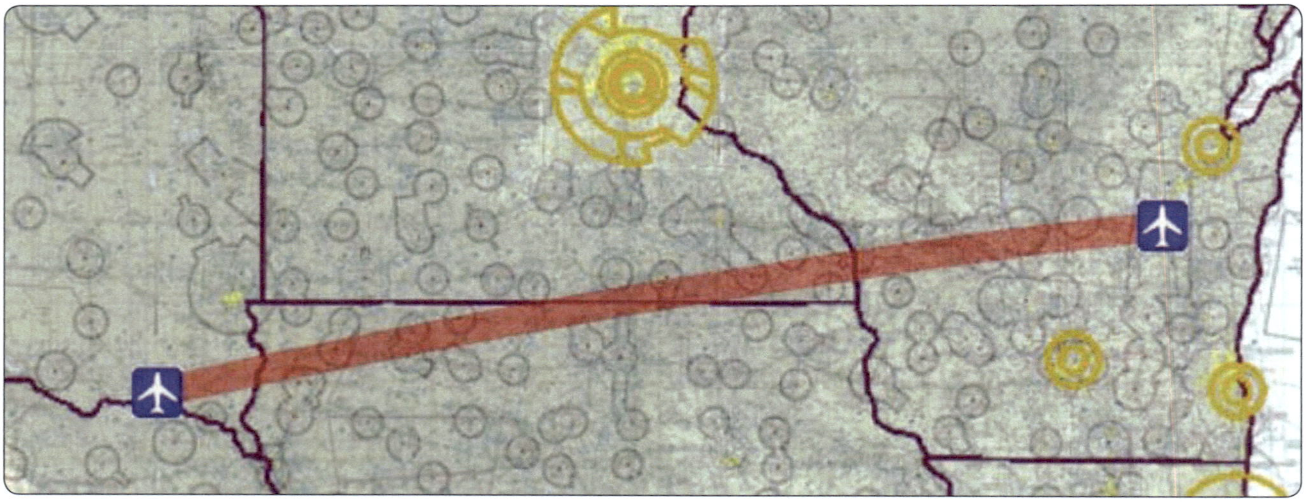

Figure D-1. *Scenario 1 chart excerpt.*

AirVenture starts on Monday, and the plan is to make the flight to OSH on Sunday. The prognostic weather charts for the next several days show that a large weather system will arrive in YKN late Saturday night from the west. It will generate a line of severe thunderstorms that move rapidly east and pass OSH late Sunday evening. Behind the front, there will be low ceilings of 300-500 feet and light to moderate rain. On Saturday, Visual Meteorological Conditions (VMC) will exist in both YKN and OSH, with the potential for isolated thunderstorms.

The pilot has logged 300 hours and has an instrument rating but has not flown in actual or simulated instrument conditions in five months. The airplane is also technically legal for IFR, although the number 2 radio is out for repair. The non-stop flight to OSH will take about 3:30, and the aircraft has 4:30 endurance with full fuel.

Scenario 2: Turboprop-Powered, Personal Transportation

The pilot owns a small specialized manufacturing firm, with production facilities in St. Petersburg, FL and a second facility in Pittsfield, MA. The pilot also has a summer home in the Berkshires. To facilitate efficient travel between these locations, the pilot owns and operates a single-engine turboprop airplane and flies as a single pilot.

It is now 10:00 am on a Friday in August after a hectic but successful new product launch in Florida. The pilot just finished a press conference and wishes to head north to enjoy the weekend in the Berkshires before meetings at the Massachusetts facility on Monday. The pilot plans to fly the PA-46 nonstop (984 NM) from St. Petersburg Clearwater (PIE) to the Pittsfield, MA airport (PSF) at FL270. [*Figure D-2*]

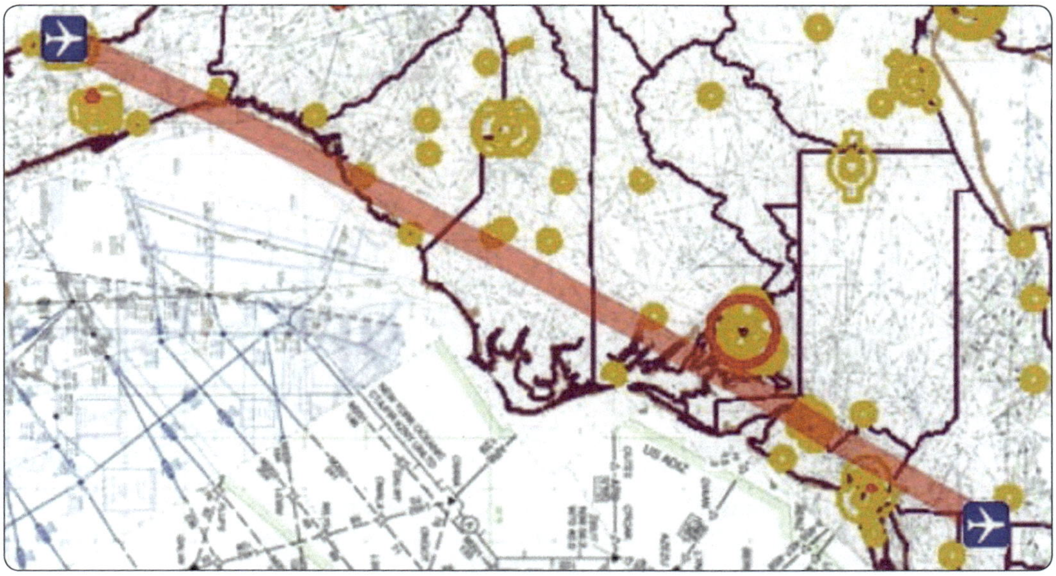

Figure D-2. *Scenario 2 chart excerpt.*

While a family member/passenger drives the pilot to the airport for an 11:00 AM takeoff, the pilot reviews the flight planning. The flight should take 3:45, and the fuel on board provides endurance of 4:45. The weather is good at PSF and en route, with isolated to scattered air mass thunderstorms. However, the pilot contemplates the air traffic in the Washington, DC and New York metro areas. In the past, reroutes occurred, and the pilot was assigned a lower altitude where the PA-46 loses fuel efficiency. The plan includes an arrival at PSF at about 3:00 PM, so the pilot and passenger may attend a party with investors at 5:00 PM.

Scenario 3: Turbine Helicopter

The pilot owns a large wholesale business with multiple warehouses throughout the Los Angeles basin in California. All these facilities are within a mile of a general aviation airport. To travel between these locations and avoid the congested freeways, the pilot flies a turbine-engine helicopter.

It is 6:00 AM Monday morning, and the pilot needs to visit four facilities. The plan includes a departure from the Santa Monica airport (SMO) and flights to Van Nuys (VNY), San Gabriel Valley (EMT), Brackett Field (POC) in Pomona, and Fullerton (FUL). The pilot plans to make the return flight to SMO in the early evening, to arrive just before sunset. *Figure D-3* shows the route of flight.

Figure D-3. *Scenario 3 chart excerpt.*

The weather throughout the basin is marginal VFR, with visibility of 3-5 miles and ceilings varying from 1,700 feet at FUL to 800 feet at POC. Clear skies are forecast after 2:00 PM. The pilot has an instrument rating, and the helicopter has IFR instrumentation, but it is not approved for IFR flight. The pilot is not instrument current. High terrain exists on the leg from SMO to VNY, although the pilot could divert to the east and fly through a pass in VMC to get to VNY.

Scenario 4: Turbojet-Powered Airplane

The pilot, based in Springfield, IL (SPI), owns a consulting firm with a nationwide clientele. The pilot flies a small turbojet airplane and uses it to get to meetings with clients. The pilot recently completed an approved training course and a type rating practical test. The pilot adds 20 percent to takeoff and landing distances as a personal minimum.

A client in Turners Falls, MA has an urgent need for a meeting tomorrow, Thursday, to evaluate some engineering plans and data. The meeting would take place in an industrial park on the Turners Falls airport (0B5). The 0B5 airport is 790 NM from SPI. The flight planning software indicates the flight will take about 2:15 and using a cruise altitude of FL350 provides a 45 minute reserve. The weather for Thursday in Massachusetts is forecast to be marginal VFR with ceilings of 1,200 feet and five miles visibility with cloud tops at 8,000 feet.

The pilot considers the destination logistics and consults both the New York sectional chart, the associated chart supplement, as well as sources for fuel, airport services, rental cars, and hotels. [*Figure D-4*]

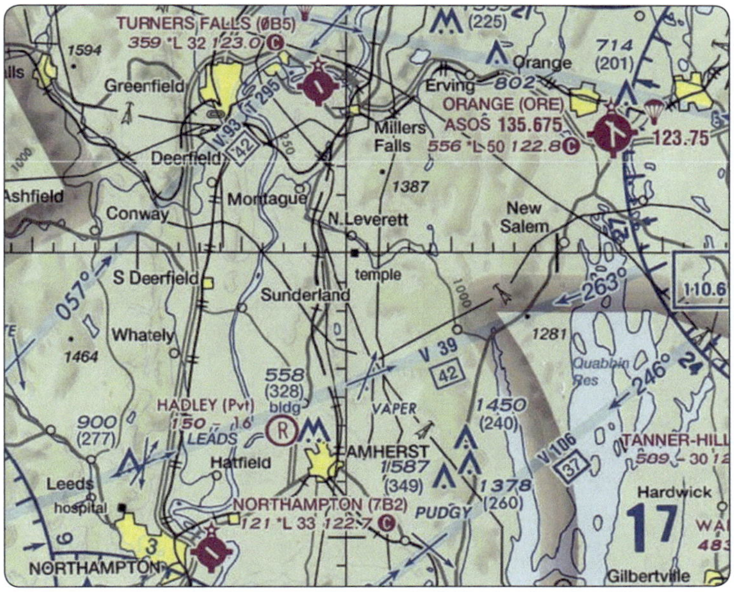

Figure D-4. *Scenario 4 chart excerpt.*

The runway at Turners Falls is 3,200 feet. Nearby airports Orange (ORE) and Northampton (7B2) have runways of 5,000 feet and 3,335 feet, respectively. The calculated unfactored landing distance is 2,760 feet at the landing weight at Turners Falls with 600 pounds of fuel remaining. The calculated unfactored takeoff distance is 2,600 feet at full fuel or 1900 feet with only 600 pounds of fuel.

After a phone discussion with the client, the pilot realizes the meeting will require 6 hours. If the departure from SPI occurs at 8:00 AM, the meeting arrival at 0B5 should take place after 11:00 AM. If the meeting ends at 5:00 PM, and the pilot flies back to SPI, the arrival there will occur sometime after 8:00 PM Thursday evening, assuming a non-stop flight. The pilot has an important meeting back in Springfield on Friday.

Turners Falls has no jet fuel, no rental cars, and only marginal hotel availability. Orange has jet fuel, but no rental cars, and no suitable lodging nearby. Northampton has no jet fuel but does have rental cars and numerous full-service hotels available. The nearest airport with all of these services is in Westfield-Barnes Regional, MA (BAF, 9,000-foot runway) about 20 miles south of Northampton.

The minimums at Orange and Westfield-Barnes Regional provide for vertical guidance through LPV minima. At Northampton, only lateral guidance (LNAV) is available with a Minimum Descent Altitude (MDA) approximately 800 feet above the ground. Only circling minimums with an MDA approximately 1,100 feet above ground is available at Turners Falls.

Glossary

#

14 CFR. *See* Title 14 of the Code of Federal Regulations.

3P. An acronym that represents the three components of the risk management cycle: Perceive, Process, Perform.

A

Acceptable risk. That part of identified risk that is allowed to persist without further engineering or management action. Making this decision is a difficult yet necessary responsibility for managing activity. This decision is made with full knowledge that it is the user who is exposed to this risk.

Aeronautical decision-making (ADM). A systematic approach to the mental process used by aircraft pilots to consistently determine the best course of action in response to a given set of circumstances.

Automatic decision-making. Quick decision-making based on experience and the expectation of a good outcome.

C

CARE. An acronym that represents the four risk assessment and mitigation elements: Consequences, Alternatives, Reality, and External pressures.

CAST/ICAO Common Taxonomy Team (CICTT). A group that developed common classifications and definitions for aviation accident and incident reporting.

Checklist. A tool that is used as a human factors aid in aviation safety. It is a systematic and sequential list of all operations that must be performed to accomplish a task properly.

Commercial Aviation Safety Team (CAST). Organization founded in 1997 to bring together various segments of the aviation community with the goal to reduce accidents through a data-driven approach.

Controlled flight into terrain (CFIT). An accident whereby an airworthy aircraft, under pilot control, inadvertently flies into terrain, an obstacle, or water.

CFR. *See* Title 14 of the Code of Federal Regulations.

Crew resource management (CRM). The application of team management concepts in the flight deck environment. CRM programs evolved to include cabin crews, maintenance personnel, and others. Pilots of small aircraft, as well as crews of larger aircraft, should make effective use of all available resources; human resources, hardware, and information. A current definition includes all groups routinely working with the flight deck crew who are involved in decisions required to operate a flight safely. These groups include, but are not limited to: pilots, dispatchers, cabin crewmembers, maintenance personnel, and air traffic controllers. CRM is one way of addressing the challenge of optimizing the human/machine interface and accompanying interpersonal activities.

Currency. Meeting all established requirements.

E

Electronic flight bag (EFB). A portable or integrated device that allows the pilot to carry all necessary aeronautical and performance data, weight and balance, and aircraft checklists in digital form and may allow remote manipulation of the avionics through wireless radio connections.

Emergency. An urgent condition or distress that requires immediate attention.

Error. Deviations from intended or expected actions that are caused by the flight crew that cause confusion, increase workload, absorb attention, reduce safety margins, increase risk, and may lead to undesired aircraft states.

External pressures. Influences external to the flight that create a sense of pressure to complete a flight—often at the expense of safety.

F

Flight management system (FMS). A system normally integrated into a technically advanced aircraft that provides an efficient means of loading and programming horizontal and vertical flight path information that can be tracked by the autopilot or followed manually by the pilot using flight director and other guidance cues.

Flight risk assessment tool (FRAT). A way to record and analyze identified hazards and risks. A FRAT can be numerical (scoring predetermined hazards) to measure risk or narrative (recording identified hazards, associate risk, and individual risk mitigations).

G

General aviation. All flights other than military and scheduled airline flights, both private and commercial.

General Aviation Joint Steering Committee (GAJSC). Team of FAA and general aviation community members formed to analyze general aviation accidents and create safety enhancements that can mitigate leading accident causes.

H

Hazard. A present condition, event, object, or circumstance that could lead to or contribute to an unplanned or undesired event, such as an accident.

Human behavior. The product of factors that cause people to act in predictable ways.

Human factors. A multidisciplinary field devoted to optimizing human performance and reducing human error. It incorporates the methods and principles of the behavioral and social sciences, engineering, and physiology. It may be described as the applied science which studies people working together in concert with machines. Human factors involve variables that influence individual performance, as well as team or crew performance.

I

Identified risk. The risk that has been determined through various analysis techniques. The first task of system safety is to identify, within practical limitations, all possible risks.

IMSAFE. An acronym that represents the six aeromedical risk areas: Illness, Medication, Stress, Alcohol, Fatigue, and Emotion.

Instrument flight rules (IFR). Rules that govern the procedure for conducting flight in weather conditions below VFR weather minimums. The term "IFR" also is used to define weather conditions and the type of flight plan under which an aircraft is operating.

Instrument meteorological conditions (IMC). Meteorological conditions expressed in terms of visibility, distance from clouds, and ceiling less than the minimums specified for visual meteorological conditions, requiring operations to be conducted under IFR.

International Civil Aviation Organization (ICAO). An international body that sets aviation safety standards. Member states agree to formulate regulation to meet those standards.

J

Judgment. The mental process of recognizing and analyzing all pertinent information in a particular situation, a rational evaluation of alternative actions in response to it, and a timely decision on which action to take.

L

Loss of control in-flight (LOC-I). An accident caused by the pilot not maintaining control of the airplane. Many LOC-I accidents are the result of stalls, spins, or accelerated maneuvers.

M

Mode annunciator. A display panel normally integrated into the primary flight display that shows the current status and operating functions of the autopilot or flight director.

Mode controller. The interface used by the pilot to select autopilot or flight director operating modes and to engage or disengage the autopilot system.

N

National Transportation Safety Board (NTSB). A United States Government independent organization responsible for investigations of accidents involving aviation, highways, waterways, pipelines, and railroads in the United States. The NTSB is charged by the Congress of the United States to investigate civil aviation accidents.

Notice to Airmen (NOTAM). A notice filed with an aviation authority to alert aircraft pilots of any hazards en route or at a specific location. The authority in turn provides means of disseminating relevant NOTAMs to pilots.

Naturalistic decision-making. *See* Automatic decision-making.

P

PAVE. An acronym that represents the four risk identification areas: Pilot, Aircraft, enVironment, and External pressures.

Personality. The embodiment of personal traits and characteristics of an individual that are set at a very early age and are extremely resistant to change.

Pilot report (PIREP). Report of meteorological phenomena encountered by aircraft.

Probable cause. The defining event that directly leads to an accident.

Proficiency. Possessing a high standard of competence or expertise.

Q

Qualification. Having the certificates, ratings, endorsements, or other designations required for the operation.

R

Residual risk. The remaining risk after system safety efforts have been fully employed. It is not necessarily the same as acceptable risk. Residual risk is the sum of acceptable risk and unidentified risk. This is the total risk passed on to the user.

Risk. The future impact of a hazard that is not eliminated or controlled.

Risk assessment. An approach to managing uncertainty. Risk assessment is a quantitative value assigned to a task, action, or event.

Risk assessment matrix. A tool used to see the relationship between risk likelihood and risk severity to determine an overall level of risk, measured as low, medium, serious, or high.

Risk likelihood. The probability of encountering risk categorized as probable, occasional, remote, or improbable.

Risk management. The part of the decision-making process which relies on situational awareness, problem recognition, and good judgment to reduce risks associated with each flight.

Risk mitigation. The process of reducing risk likelihood and severity to lower levels.

Risk severity. The magnitude of consequences of risk categorized as catastrophic, critical, marginal, or negligible.

Root cause. The underlying reason that leads the pilot or aircraft toward the probable cause of an accident.

S

Safety management system (SMS). The application of special technical and managerial skills to the systematic, forward-looking identification and control of hazards throughout the life cycle of a project, program, or activity.

Single-pilot resource management (SRM). The art/science of managing all the resources (both on board the aircraft and from outside sources) available to a single pilot (before and during flight) to ensure that the successful outcome of the flight is never in doubt.

Situational awareness. Perception of variables in the environment, comprehension of their meaning, and projection of their status in the near future.

Stress. The body's response to demands placed upon it.

System component failure of the powerplant (SCF-PP). An accident caused by failure of an engine component that may lead to complete failure of the engine.

T

TEAM (or TEMA). An acronym that represents the four risk mitigation process steps: Transfer, Eliminate, Accept, and Mitigate (or Transfer, Eliminate, Mitigate, and Accept).

Technically advanced airplane (TAA). An airplane equipped with an electronically advanced avionics system.

Threat. Hazards present in the environment or that are outside the influence of the flight crew that increase operational complexity and may lead to errors.

Threat and error management (TEM). A risk management methodology designed to anticipate and prevent threats from creating errors, trap errors before they cause undesired aircraft states, and mitigate undesired aircraft states to stop an incident or accident from occurring.

Total risk. The sum of identified and unidentified risks.

Title 14 of the Code of Federal Regulations (14 CFR). Includes what was formerly known as the Federal Aviation Regulations governing the operation of aircraft, airways, and airmen.

U

Unacceptable risk. The risk that cannot be tolerated by the managing activity. It is a subset of identified risk that must be eliminated or controlled.

Unidentified risk. Risk not yet identified. Some unidentified risks are subsequently identified when a mishap occurs. Some risk is never known.

Undesirable risk. A tolerable risk that must be prepared for and mitigated as best as possible.

V

Visual flight rules (VFR). Code of Federal Regulations that govern the procedures for conducting flight under visual conditions.

Visual meteorological conditions (VMC). Meteorological conditions expressed in terms of visibility, distance from cloud, and ceiling meeting or exceeding the minimums specified for VFR.

Index

Symbols

A

C

D

E

F

H

I

L

N

P

R

S

T

V

W

Made in the USA
Columbia, SC
03 January 2024

29791603R00043